"But ye shall receive power,
after that the Holy Ghost is
come upon you: and ye shall
be witnesses unto me both in
Jerusalem, and in all Judea,
and in Samaria, and unto
the uttermost part of the
earth" (Acts 1:8).

Acts

of the

HOLY SPIRIT

When You Long To Experience the New Testament Power of the Holy Spirit in Your Life TODAY!

By Marilyn Hickey

ACTS of the HOLY SPIRIT
When You Long To Experience the New Testament Power of the Holy Spirit in Your Life TODAY!

ISBN 1-56441-023-4

Printed in the United States of America
All scriptures are quoted from the *King James* version of the Bible.

CONTENTS

ACTS

Introduction

Imagine the apostles' distress—the physical body of Jesus was ascending out of their sight! For 3½ years God had been manifested in the flesh-and-blood body of Jesus Christ. The evidence for His divinity was compelling: men raised from the dead, blind eyes opened, deaf ears unstopped, the crippled walking, lepers cleansed, 5,000 fed, and even a walk on the water. Added to all of this was Jesus' unchallengeable teaching about the kingdom of God which left even His enemies dumbfounded. But now the body in which He "*. . . began both to do and teach*" (Acts 1:1) was vanishing into the clouds!

Jesus, of course, did not cease to exist; but for our sake His physical body ascended out of view to make way for the new, corporate Body in which He would continue "*. . . to do and teach.*" That Body is His Church—much like the burning bush of the Old Testament, burning yet unconsumed. God had spoken to Moses from the burning bush (Exodus 3); and now, 1500 years later, God wanted to

7

speak to all the world through the burning bush which was His Church. The miracles and teachings of Jesus were to continue until the end of the age when Jesus returned.

The outpouring of the Holy Spirit at Pentecost, according to Acts 1:8, was to empower those who were present in the Upper Room to be Jesus' witnesses "... *in Jerusalem, and in all Judea, and in Samaria, and unto the uttermost part of the earth." Witness* means "an evidence." Although Jesus Who was the physical evidence of God's existence was gone, NOW the witness or evidence for the fact of Jesus' resurrection and the Spirit's outpouring was to be seen in the lives of those who were indwelt with the Lord's very own life. The world was now to behold Jesus in His many-membered Body.

The true Body of Christ will always present supernatural phenomena to the world—just as Jesus did. When Peter stood up to preach after having received the Holy Spirit, the man who had been fearful and cringing just days earlier suddenly was a prophet, apostle, and evangelist with the fire of God in his heart. Peter was certainly a witness or evidence that what Jesus had begun while in His physical body was continuing—in this instance through a Galilean fisherman.

Jesus' ministry had been characterized by prayer, and in Acts chapter 3 we see His habit of prayer being continued through two members of His new Body—Peter and John. This chapter also records a marvelous miracle performed in Jerusalem. Remember, Jesus had said that His followers would be witnesses *first* in Jerusalem.

Introduction

But the Lord had said that His disciples were to be witnesses in Judea, Samaria, and unto the uttermost parts of the earth. Would the miracles and message of Jesus travel no farther than the Jewish community in Israel's capital city? No! Just as Jesus had spoken, the burning bush, with its good news, began to spread its flames to Judea:

> *There came also a multitude out of the cities round about unto Jerusalem, bringing sick folks, and them which were vexed with unclean spirits: and they were healed every one* (Acts 5:16).

Hallelujah! They were "healed every one." The disciples confirmed the fact that they had truly received the same life and power which worked through Jesus to heal the sick. This was solid evidence that the Cross had not ended what Jesus came to do and to teach! Multitudes beheld Jesus in a new way—now Jesus was in Jerusalem *and* Judea at the same time—as His disciples used "the name" to bring healing and salvation to all in both regions who believed the good news.

Watch out, Samaria; the fire is coming your way! A persecution against the church in Jerusalem helped spread the gospel witness. As a result Philip, a deacon, went to Samaria and "preached Christ unto them" (Acts 8:5). The teaching ministry of Jesus was carried on not this time by an apostle, a prophet, or one of the twelve but by a deacon (one who serves) within the Church. And could this "server" also be an evidence of Christ's continuing miracle power? Yes! Acts 8:6 records, *"And the people with one accord gave heed unto those things which Philip spake, hearing and seeing the miracles which he did."*

The book of Acts shows us that we shouldn't limit the miraculous to the "big names" within the Church. There is only one big name—the name of JESUS! And you and I are living proof that He is still alive.

It was granted to Paul, once the great persecutor of the Church, to take the miracles and teachings of Jesus unto the "ends of the earth" (Acts 13:47). Were Paul and Barnabas proof to the gentiles of Christ's reality? Of course they were; they spoke boldly, and God *". . . granted signs and wonders to be done by their hands"* (Acts 14:3).

The Acts of the Holy Spirit through the Church continues *today* in you and me. We are God's burning bush—on fire, but never consumed. Internal and external pressures may try to smother this flame, but God's Spirit burns eternally in the hearts of men and women who have been born again. The book of Acts is the story of how this flame began, how it overcame every attempt to put out its light, and its victorious spread throughout all the earth.

THE AUTHOR

We know from their prologues that Luke was the author of both the gospel that bears his name and the book of Acts:

Forasmuch as many have taken in hand to set forth in order a declaration of those things which

*are most surely believed among us, It seemed good
to me also, having had perfect understanding of
all things from the very first, to write unto thee
in order, most excellent Theophilus* (Luke 1:1,3).

*The former treatise have I made, O Theophilus,
of all that Jesus began both to do and teach*
(Acts 1:1).

Luke means "light-giving." He was a physician:

Luke, the beloved physician, and Demas, greet you
(Colossians 4:14).

We first encounter Luke in the book of Acts in the story
which takes place in Troas. It was there that he first began
to use the term *we* in his account:

*And after he had seen the vision, immediately we
endeavoured to go into Macedonia, assuredly
gathering that the Lord had called us for to preach
the gospel unto them. Therefore loosing from
Troas, we came with a straight course to
Samothracia, and the next day to Neapolis*
(Acts 16:10,11).

Paul's mention of three friends who were "of the
circumcision" in the book of Colossians, followed by his
mention of Luke later on (see Colossians 4:10-14), suggests
that Luke was a gentile. He may have been one of Paul's
converts. As a gentile, Luke is the only non-Jewish writer
in the New Testament. Luke stayed with Paul throughout

his ministry, even through the rough times of Paul's imprisonments. Writing during his second Roman imprisonment, Paul said, *"Only Luke is with me. . . . "* (II Timothy 4:11).

Luke's careful investigation, eyewitness accounts, and Holy Spirit inspired writing give us a marvelous glimpse of the early Church—its birth, its growth, its trials, and its triumphs!

CHAPTER ONE

Special Delivery —the Church's Birthday
(Acts 1:3-2:4)

I f you've ever been present at a birth, you know the awe and wonder at the entrance into this world of a newborn! What emotion! What joy! Imagine your heavenly Father's joy at the birth of the Church—something planned by the Trinity in eternity past and looked forward to for centuries. However, the descent of the Holy Spirit to birth the Church required the ascension of the One Who had said, " . . . *I will build my church; and the gates of hell shall not prevail against it*" (Matthew 16:18). The Spirit could not be sent because Jesus had not been glorified:

> *In the last day, that great day of the feast, Jesus stood and cried, saying, If any man thirst, let him come unto me, and drink. He that believeth on me, as the scripture hath said, out of his belly shall flow rivers of living water. (But this spake he of the Spirit, which they that believe on him should receive: for the Holy Ghost was not yet*

13

given; because that Jesus was not yet glorified.)
(John 7:37-39).

Jesus had told His disciples of the necessity for His return to the Father:

Nevertheless I tell you the truth; It is expedient for you that I go away: for if I go not away, the Comforter will not come unto you; but if I depart, I will send him unto you (John 16:7).

Luke had briefly (in only one verse—Luke 24:51) touched on the Ascension in his former letter, but now he elaborates on Jesus' activities following the Resurrection:

To whom also he shewed himself alive after his passion by many infallible proofs, being seen of them forty days, and speaking of the things pertaining to the kingdom of God (Acts 1:3).

Let's look at these *"infallible proofs"* of Christ's resurrection:

Jesus appeared to Mary Magdalene:

Now when Jesus was risen early the first day of the week, he appeared first to Mary Magdalene, out of whom he had cast seven devils (Mark 16:9).

Jesus appeared to other women:

And as they went to tell his disciples, behold,

*Jesus met them, saying, All hail. And they came
and held him by the feet, and worshipped him*
(Matthew 28:9).

Jesus appeared to Peter:

*Saying, The Lord is risen indeed, and hath
appeared to Simon* (Luke 24:34).

Jesus appeared to two men on the road to Emmaus:

*And it came to pass, that, while they communed
together and reasoned, Jesus himself drew near,
and went with them* (Luke 24:15).

Jesus appeared to ten disciples:

*Then the same day at evening, being the first day
of the week, when the doors were shut where the
disciples were assembled for fear of the Jews,
came Jesus and stood in the midst, and saith
unto them, Peace be unto you. But Thomas, one
of the twelve, called Didymus, was not with them
when Jesus came* (John 20:19,24).

Jesus appeared to all eleven disciples:

*And after eight days again his disciples were
within, and Thomas with them: then came Jesus,
the doors being shut, and stood in the midst,
and said, Peace be unto you* (John 20:26).

Jesus appeared to seven disciples by the sea:

After these things Jesus shewed himself again to the disciples at the sea of Tiberias, and on this wise shewed he himself (John 21:1).

Jesus appeared to the disciples on a mountain:

Then the eleven disciples went away into Galilee, into a mountain where Jesus had appointed them. And when they saw him, they worshipped him: but some doubted (Matthew 28:16,17).

Jesus appeared to the disciples (including Matthias) at His ascension:

And it came to pass, while he blessed them, he was parted from them, and carried up into heaven (Luke 24:51).

Wherefore of these men which have companied with us all the time that the Lord Jesus went in and out among us, Beginning from the baptism of John, unto that same day that he was taken up from us, must one be ordained to be a witness with us of his resurrection. And they gave forth their lots; and the lot fell upon Matthias; and he was numbered with the eleven apostles (Acts 1:21,22,26).

Jesus appeared to over 500 people:

After that, he was seen of above five hundred brethren at once; of whom the greater part remain unto this present, but some are fallen asleep (I Corinthians 15:6).

Jesus appeared to His half-brother James:

After that, he was seen of James; then of all the apostles (I Corinthians 15:7).

There are also at least three post-ascension appearances of Jesus:

Jesus appeared to Stephen:

But he [Stephen], *being full of the Holy Ghost, looked up stedfastly into heaven, and saw the glory of God, and Jesus standing on the right hand of God* (Acts 7:55).

Jesus appeared to Paul:

And last of all he was seen of me also, as of one born out of due time (I Corinthians 15:8).

Jesus appeared to John on the isle of Patmos:

And I turned to see the voice that spake with me. And being turned, I saw seven golden candlesticks; And in the midst of the seven candlesticks one like unto the Son of man, . . . (Revelation 1:12,13).

PREPARATION FOR THE SPIRIT'S INDWELLING

For 40 days after His resurrection, Jesus came and went among His followers. He was no doubt preparing them for the time when they would no longer have His physical presence in their midst. They would soon know Him in an entirely different way:

> *And I will pray the Father, and he shall give you another Comforter, that he may abide with you for ever: Even the Spirit of truth; whom the world cannot receive, because it seeth him not, neither knoweth him: but ye know him; for he dwelleth with you, and shall be in you. I will not leave you comfortless: I will come to you. At that day ye shall know that I am in my Father, and ye in me, and I in you* (John 14:16-18,20).

> *Wherefore henceforth know we no man after the flesh: yea, though we have known Christ after the flesh, yet now henceforth know we him no more* (II Corinthians 5:16).

This baptism of the Holy Spirit was one of the " . . . *things pertaining to the kingdom of God*" (Acts 1:3) that Jesus spoke about before His departure in the clouds. This was not the first time He had instructed His disciples concerning the promised Holy Spirit:

And, being assembled together with them, commanded them that they should not depart from Jerusalem, but wait for the promise of the Father, which, saith he, ye have heard of me (Acts 1:4).

John the Baptist had also foretold of this Holy Spirit baptism:

And [John] *preached, saying, There cometh one mightier than I after me, the latchet of whose shoes I am not worthy to stoop down and unloose. I indeed have baptized you with water: but he shall baptize you with the Holy Ghost* (Mark 1:7,8).

Notice that the Church would begin where Christ was crucified: Jerusalem. The place of cursing was to become the place of blessing. The curse would be turned to a blessing on the day of Pentecost.

Whenever I read this first chapter of Acts, I am encouraged! Why? Because whenever I read about the disciples and their question to Jesus in verse 6, I know there are never any stupid questions as far as God is concerned! Jesus had just spent 40 days speaking to them about the things pertaining to the kingdom, and yet they were *still* unclear about God's program for the Jews and gentiles:

When they therefore were come together, they asked of him, saying, Lord, wilt thou at this time restore again the kingdom to Israel? And he said unto them, It is not for you to know the times or

19

the seasons, which the Father hath put in his own power (Acts 1:6,7).

Jesus was *so* patient with them. He didn't slap His forehead and moan, "I can't believe it! What have I been talking about these past 40 days? Haven't you been listening?" No, instead He gently told them not to worry about the timing of the kingdom. He turned their attention to something of more immediate importance:

> *But ye shall receive power, after that the Holy Ghost is come upon you: and ye shall be witnesses unto me both in Jerusalem, and in all Judea, and in Samaria, and unto the uttermost part of the earth* (Acts 1:8).

The timing of the kingdom was the Father's business; the witnessing with power to the uttermost part of the earth was the disciples' business. This power was *dunamis* in the Greek language—*miracle-working power.* This was the kind of power necessary to take the good news throughout the earth.

These were Jesus' last recorded words while on earth. Last words are usually the most important. If I'm leaving to go to the store or to visit a friend, my last words to my husband are the ones I want him to remember most: "Don't forget to turn off the stove"; "Don't forget to let the dog out." The most important subject on Jesus' mind before He ascended was the miracle-working power He was going to send upon His disciples.

THE ASCENSION

Having said His parting words, Jesus returned to the glory He had left some 33 years earlier:

> *And when he had spoken these things, while they beheld, he was taken up; and a cloud received him out of their sight* (Acts 1:9).

> *And now, O Father, glorify thou me with thine own self with the glory which I had with thee before the world was* (John 17:5).

> *Who* [Jesus], *being in the form of God, thought it not robbery to be equal with God: But made himself of no reputation, and took upon him the form of a servant, and was made in the likeness of men* (Philippians 2:6,7).

Imagine the emotions experienced by those disciples who stood watching Jesus leave their sight! This was the One Who had been their leader for three-and-a-half years; He had stilled the storm on the Sea of Galilee, fed the multitudes, raised the dead, and healed the sick. This One Who spoke and acted like no other in the history of man was no longer going to be physically present with them. No doubt the disciples, despite the promise of the Holy Spirit, felt an emptiness and a loss that, if not checked, would have overwhelmed them. Their heavenly Father graciously provided a word of encouragement and comfort to them through two angels standing nearby:

21

And while they looked stedfastly toward heaven as he went up, behold, two men stood by them in white apparel; Which also said, Ye men of Galilee, why stand ye gazing up into heaven? this same Jesus, which is taken up from you into heaven, shall so come in like manner as ye have seen him go into heaven (Acts 1:10,11).

This is not the first time we see two witnesses; there were two witnesses on the Mount of Transfiguration:

And it came to pass about an eight days after these sayings, he took Peter and John and James, and went up into a mountain to pray. And as he prayed, the fashion of his countenance was altered, and his raiment was white and glistering. And, behold, there talked with him two men, which were Moses and Elias (Luke 9:28-30).

There were two witnesses at Jesus' tomb:

Now upon the first day of the week, very early in the morning, they came unto the sepulchre, bringing the spices which they had prepared, and certain others with them. And it came to pass, as they were much perplexed thereabout, behold, two men stood by them in shining garments (Luke 24:1,4).

Jesus sent out the disciples two-by-two:

*And he called unto him the twelve, and began to
send them forth by two and two; and gave them
power over unclean spirits* (Mark 6:7).

Two has always been the required number of
confirmation:

*One witness shall not rise up against a man for
any iniquity, or for any sin, in any sin that he
sinneth: at the mouth of two witnesses, or at the
mouth of three witnesses, shall the matter be
established* (Deuteronomy 19:15).

Two is YOUR number for power:

*Again I say unto you, That if two of you shall
agree on earth as touching any thing that they
shall ask, it shall be done for them of my Father
which is in heaven* (Matthew 18:19).

Even on the Mercy Seat we see the number two:

*And thou shalt make two cherubims of gold, of
beaten work shalt thou make them, in the two
ends of the mercy seat* (Exodus 25:18).

A REPLACEMENT FOR JUDAS

Following the Ascension the disciples returned to the
Upper Room in Jerusalem (see the map on page 214). This

was in obedience to the Lord's command:

> *And, being assembled together with them,* [Jesus]
> *commanded them that they should not depart*
> *from Jerusalem, but wait for the promise of the*
> *Father, which, saith he, ye have heard of me*
> (Acts 1:4).

Obedience always results in blessing! The Holy Spirit wasn't going to be sent to Rome, to Samaria, or to any location outside of Jerusalem. Anyone who chose to ignore the Lord's words, to spiritualize them away, would miss out on the initial outpouring of the promised Comforter and "dunamis" power that would turn the world upside down.

Evidently the eleven disciples took up temporary residence in the Upper Room; verse 13 tells us they "abode" there at this time. Jesus had told them to "wait" for the promise of the Father. This waiting lasted about ten days and was a time of prayer:

> *These all continued with one accord in prayer*
> *and supplication, with the women, and Mary the*
> *mother of Jesus, and with his brethren* (Acts 1:14).

The Greek word for "continued" means *persevered*. They persevered with one purpose in prayer. Don't you know that those believers were precious to the Lord; they were the small handful of *seed* that God was going to use to *sow* the gospel into all the world. The *harvest* would stretch over two thousand years and include you and me!

Those waiting in the Upper Room included Jesus' mother and *brethren.* The Greek word used here means "of the same womb." These "brethren" were literally half-brothers to Jesus. These were the same "brethren" who earlier had not believed that Jesus was the Messiah:

For neither did his brethren believe in him (John 7:5).

Obviously His family did a turnaround. They all persevered in the Upper Room, waiting to receive the baptism of the Holy Spirit—Mary included. This verse has been used to bring revival in South America. Why? Because many of the people in those countries worship Mary. The missionaries have found that the best question to ask the people is, "Do you really love Mary?"

"Oh, yes. We really love Mary."

"Would you like to do what Mary did?"

"Oh, yes. We'd love to do what Mary did."

And so the missionaries share Acts 1:14 with the people, show them how Mary was in the room with the others who were baptized in the Holy Spirit, and lead them to the Lord and the baptism of the Holy Spirit! Some of the Full Gospel churches in Brazil have ten thousand members or more, and it started with following Mary's example.

The first order of business in those days was the selection of Judas' replacement. Some people say that the disciples were out of God's will to choose Matthias since Paul was called to be an apostle. But the Bible never says that. We know from reading Ephesians 4:11 and 12 that there is an apostolic ministry throughout the Church age:

> *And he gave some, apostles; and some, prophets; and some evangelists; and some, pastors and teachers; For the perfecting of the saints, for the work of the ministry, for the edifying of the body of Christ* (Ephesians 4:11,12).

There were originally 12 apostles, and their names will be on the 12 foundation stones of the new Jerusalem along with the names of the 12 tribes on the gates:

> *And had a wall great and high, and had twelve gates, and at the gates twelve angels, and names written thereon, which are the names of the twelve tribes of the children of Israel: And the wall of the city had twelve foundations, and in them the names of the twelve apostles of the Lamb* (Revelation 21:12,14).

I think Matthias is the twelfth foundation stone because Paul was the apostle to the gentiles, not the Jews. The foundation stones of the new Jerusalem parallel the stones that the high priests wore over their hearts; they are Jewish in character. Even Paul disqualified himself from being one of the original apostles:

> *And last of all he was seen of me also, as of one born out of due time* (I Corinthians 15:8).

Remember that the disciples hadn't received the indwelling Holy Spirit yet, so they had to rely on the God-ordained method of casting lots. In the Old Testament the high priests had the Urim and Thummim, which they cast into their laps. *Urim* and *Thummim* means "lights and perfection." To know God's light and His perfect will for any given situation, the high priest cast the lots:

> *The lot is cast into the lap; but the whole disposing thereof is of the LORD* (Proverbs 16:33).

The Bible is clear that the Holy Spirit's choice to replace Judas was Matthias:

> *And they gave forth their lots; and the lot fell upon Matthias; and he was numbered with the eleven apostles* (Acts 1:26).

We never read of Matthias after this, but neither do we read of some of the other apostles.

THE CHURCH IS BORN

For 1500 years, every 50th day following the offering of the barley sheaf at the Feast of Unleavened Bread (part of the larger celebration of Passover), the Israelites celebrated the Feast of Weeks or the Feast of Harvest (called *Pentecost*—Greek for "fifty"). The Jews trace their first Pentecost back to the giving of the Law on Mt. Sinai—the birthplace and birthday of Judaism. The New Testament Pentecost was the birthday of Christianity. Paul compares and contrasts these two Pentecosts in II Corinthians chapter 3. Let's take a look at them:

OLD TESTAMENT PENTECOST	NEW TESTAMENT PENTECOST
The 50th day	The 50th day
Writing of Ten Commandments on two tables of stone	Writing of commandments of love on tables of the heart and mind
By the finger of God	By the Spirit of God
Three thousand people slain	Three thousand people live
A ministration of death	A ministration of life
The letter	The Spirit
Glory on the face of Moses	Glory on the face of Jesus
Face veiled so people could not behold the glory	Unveiled face so we can be changed into the same glory
Glory to be done away	Glory that remains
Ministers of Old Covenant	Ministers of the New Covenant
Mt. Sinai	Mt. Zion

Pentecost was the celebration of harvesttime; it was marked by the waving of two loaves of bread by the priest:

> *And ye shall count unto you from the morrow after the sabbath, from the day that ye brought the sheaf of the wave offering; seven sabbaths shall be complete: Even unto the morrow after the seventh sabbath shall ye number fifty days; and ye shall offer a new meat [meal] offering unto the LORD. Ye shall bring out of your habitations two wave loaves of two tenth deals: they shall be of fine flour; they shall be baken with leaven; they are the firstfruits unto the LORD*
> (Leviticus 23:15-17).

The two loaves of bread certainly represent the two peoples—Jews and gentiles—who will compose the Lord's Body. Pentecost shows us that we are part of the end-time harvest and the end-time outpouring of God's Spirit.

Acts 2:1-4 are familiar verses to many people—especially those in Pentecostal or charismatic churches. Let's look at these four verses one at a time:

> *And when the day of Pentecost was fully come,*
> *they were all with one accord in one place*
> (Acts 2:1).

Jesus had started with 12 disciples; now there were 120 waiting in the Upper Room. These were waiting "with one accord." Many times today churches lack the power of the Holy Spirit because they are in *dis*cord rather than *one accord.* The prayer and unity of this group set the stage for the Holy Spirit's arrival—which was accompanied by two outward manifestations:

> *And suddenly there came a sound from heaven*
> *as of a rushing mighty wind, and it filled all the*
> *house where they were sitting. And there*
> *appeared unto them cloven tongues like as of fire,*
> *and it sat upon each of them* (Acts 2:2,3).

Both the sense of sound and the sense of sight were involved in this event. There were actually three signs given as a witness to the Spirit's arrival: the mighty rushing wind, the cloven tongues like as fire, and the speaking with other tongues.

Wind and *fire* were familiar Old Testament symbols of God's Spirit:

> *Then said he unto me, Prophesy unto the wind, prophesy, son of man, and say to the wind, Thus saith the Lord* GOD; *Come from the four winds, O breath, and breathe upon these slain, that they may live. And ye shall know that I am the* LORD, *when I have opened your graves, O my people, and brought you up out of your graves, And shall put my spirit in you, and ye shall live,* . . . (Ezekiel 37:9,13,14).

> *And mount Sinai was altogether on a smoke, because the* LORD *descended upon it in fire: and the smoke thereof ascended as the smoke of a furnace, and the whole mount quaked greatly* (Exodus 19:18).

The Church began with "a sound from heaven," and it will end with a sound from heaven:

> *For the Lord himself shall descend from heaven with a shout, with the voice of the archangel, and with the trump of God: and the dead in Christ shall rise first* (I Thessalonians 4:16).

The first sound from heaven on the day of Pentecost brought the filling of the Holy Spirit:

> *And they were all filled with the Holy Ghost, and*

began to speak with other tongues, as the Spirit gave them utterance (Acts 2:4).

THE FREE GIFT

This was the promise of the Father mentioned by Jesus in Acts 1:8. It was not given on the basis of works or "tarrying." We are saved by grace, and we receive the Holy Spirit by grace. People say, "I'm not good enough to receive the Holy Spirit yet." I say it is the other way around: You receive the Holy Spirit, and He makes you better.

One time I was teaching in a night service. After the service some young couples came up to me and asked if I could go out to coffee with them. Normally I don't do that. I didn't know them. But I felt very much in my heart that I was supposed to go. There were about six couples, and they had some Bible questions they wanted to ask me.

One young man said "I've never been filled with the Spirit. My father's a Spirit-filled pastor, but you know I've never been good enough to receive the baptism of the Holy Spirit. Some day I will get good enough and I will receive. I really want to—I'm really hungry."

I told him the Bible says you can receive as soon as you ask. He said he didn't think it said that. I gave him some scriptures, among them this one:

If ye then, being evil, know how to give good gifts unto your children: how much more shall your

heavenly Father give the Holy Spirit to them that
ask him? (Luke 11:13).

I told him he could be Spirit-filled right there in that restaurant. He said he wouldn't do that right there; he wanted to go out in the parking lot. So we went to the parking lot, and he received the baptism of the Holy Spirit! The "promise of the Father" is a gift, and we can receive Him as soon as faith comes.

We'll see that in Acts 10; Cornelius and his household didn't "get good enough." They heard the Word—faith comes by hearing the Word—and they were Spirit-filled.

The fire has now been ignited; the waiting is over. The Church is aglow with the Spirit and empowered to be "witnesses" to the fact of Christ's resurrection and ascension. The Church is God's *evidence* that sin and death have been conquered through the life and death of Israel's Messiah. This gospel or "good news" will be followed with signs and wonders wherever it goes.

But there are storm clouds on the horizon trying to gather strength enough to douse this fire before it grows large enough to consume everything in its path. God's *burning bush*, however, is fed by His very life—a life that, as we shall see, is well able to meet every challenge to its existence.

CHAPTER TWO

No Wimps!—the Church Receives Power
(Acts 2:5-4:31)

You can never understand the New Testament without first knowing the Old Testament. For example, we're told in verse 5 of chapter 2 that there were Jews from "every nation under heaven" living (and no doubt visiting) in Jerusalem around the day of Pentecost. Why would these Jews be out of every nation under heaven? Why hadn't they lived in Israel all their lives? What brought them to Jerusalem at this time of year?

For the answers, we have to go back to the books of Exodus and Leviticus. When the Israelites were first delivered from Egypt, God commanded them to keep three national holidays or feasts:

> *Three times thou shalt keep a feast unto me in the year. Thou shalt keep the feast of unleavened bread* [Passover]: *(thou shalt eat unleavened bread seven days, as I commanded thee, in the time appointed*

of the month Abib; for in it thou camest out from
Egypt: and none shall appear before me empty:)
And the feast of harvest [Pentecost], *the firstfruits*
of thy labours, which thou hast sown in the
field: and the feast of ingathering [Tabernacles],
which is in the end of the year, when thou hast
gathered in thy labours out of the field
(Exodus 23:14-16).

The Jews couldn't celebrate these holidays just anywhere; God chose *Jerusalem* as the site for the feasts:

Three times in a year shall all thy males appear
before the LORD thy God in the place which he
shall choose; . . . (Deuteronomy 16:16).

Once the Israelites were settled in the Promised Land and Jerusalem became the center of worship, these three feasts were the highlights of the Jewish year—until the kingdom split after Solomon's death and the people of the divided kingdoms were eventually carried away as captives to Assyria and Babylon. When these captivities ended and the Jews were allowed to return to Israel, many chose to remain scattered abroad. Others took advantage of business opportunities in foreign soil and moved in small groups throughout the Mediterranean area and the Middle East. But God's commandment to celebrate the three feast days in Jerusalem never changed; thus the Jewish communities that had sprung up outside of Israel had "devout men" who traveled to Jerusalem during Passover, Pentecost, and Tabernacles.

This "multitude" of multilingual Jews had come to Jerusalem to celebrate Passover, and they stayed the 50 day interval before Pentecost rather than go all the way home and come back. The map on page 215 shows the geographical extent of this multitude:

> *Parthians, and Medes, and Elamites, and the dwellers in Mesopotamia, and in Judea, and Cappadocia, in Pontus, and Asia, Phrygia, and Pamphylia, in Egypt, and in the parts of Libya about Cyrene, and strangers of Rome, Jews and proselytes, Cretes, and Arabians, . . .*
> (Acts 2:9-11).

Our God is so economical! He took this perfect opportunity to birth His Church and to spread the news of His Son's death and resurrection, and He did it through the gift of tongues given to a group of "ignorant" Galileans:

> *And they were all filled with the Holy Ghost, and began to speak with other tongues, as the Spirit gave them utterance. Now when this was noised abroad, the multitude came together, and were confounded, because that every man heard them speak in his own language. And they were all amazed and marvelled, saying one to another, Behold, are not all these which speak Galileans? And how hear we every man in our own tongue, wherein we were born?* (Acts 2:4, 6-8).

We know from verse 11 what was spoken in tongues:

> *. . . we do hear them speak in our tongues the*
> *wonderful works of God* (Acts 2:11).

The expression "wonderful works" can be translated "great things," and it is used only one other time in the New Testament. Mary sang it concerning God's goodness in choosing her to be the earthly mother of Jesus:

> *For he that is mighty hath done to me great*
> *things; and holy is his name* (Luke 1:49).

The disciples no doubt shared the *great things* about the life, death, and resurrection of the Lord Jesus. This supernatural occurrence of speaking in tongues resulted in three reactions: some were amazed and acknowledged God's supernatural manifestation; others doubted and questioned; still others mocked, accusing the disciples of being drunk. It is the same today! Some come to our meetings and say, "This is supernatural; God is speaking to me"; others say, "I don't know about all this speaking in tongues; I kinda doubt it"; and still others openly mock and declare that "Tongues aren't for today!"

PETER'S FIRST SERMON

Now that God had everyone's attention, He was ready to fulfill Jesus' promise that the disciples would "receive power" once the Holy Spirit had come upon them. Peter, the disciple who had denied Jesus three times and gone back fishing following the Ascension, was the first instrument

God chose to use under the anointing of the newly poured out Holy Spirit:

> *But Peter, standing up with the eleven, lifted up his voice, and said unto them, Ye men of Judea, and all ye that dwell at Jerusalem, be this known unto you, and hearken to my words* (Acts 2:14).

Notice that Peter was standing with the other eleven—including Matthias. Rather than the disciples being drunk at only nine o'clock in the morning, Peter arrests the Jewish crowd's attention by soberly referring to a prophecy which was no doubt well-known to his listeners: *"But this is that which was spoken by the prophet Joel"* (Acts 2:16):

PETER	JOEL
And it shall come to pass in the last days, saith God, I will pour out of my Spirit upon all flesh: and your sons and your daughters shall prophesy, and your young men shall see visions and your old men shall dream dreams: And on my servants and on my handmaidens I will pour out in those days of my Spirit; and they shall prophesy: And I will shew wonders in heaven above,	*And it shall come to pass afterward, that I will pour out my spirit upon all flesh; and your sons and your daughters shall prophesy, your old men shall dream dreams, your young men shall see visions: And also upon the servants and upon the handmaids in those days will I pour out my spirit. And I will shew wonders in the heavens and in the earth, blood, and fire, and pillars of smoke. The sun*

and signs in the earth beneath; blood, and fire, and vapour of smoke: The sun shall be turned into darkness, and the moon into blood, before that great and notable day of the Lord come: And it shall come to pass that whosoever shall call on the name of the Lord shall be saved (Acts 2:17-21).

shall be turned into darkness, and the moon into blood, before the great and the terrible day of the LORD come. And it shall come to pass, that whosoever shall call on the name of the LORD shall be delivered: for in mount Zion and in Jerusalem shall be deliverance, as the LORD hath said, and in remnant whom the LORD shall call (Joel 2:28-32).

How could this fisherman recite from memory such a large portion from a minor prophet like Joel? Jesus had promised them that such would be the case:

And ye shall be brought before governors and kings for my sake, for a testimony against them and the Gentiles. But when they deliver you up, take no thought how or what ye shall speak: for it shall be given you in that same hour what ye shall speak. For it is not ye that speak, but the Spirit of your Father which speaketh in you (Matthew 10:18-20).

Once Peter had captured the crowd's attention through Joel's prophecy, he quickly got to the heart of his message (recorded in Acts 2:22-24).

• Jesus was a man approved of God.

• They crucified Jesus, but that was according to God's plan.

• God raised Jesus from the dead.

Peter again quoted from the Bible—this time from David's Messianic psalm (Psalms 16:8-11):

> *For David speaketh concerning him, I foresaw the Lord always before my face, for he is on my right hand, that I should not be moved: Therefore did my heart rejoice, and my tongue was glad; moreover also my flesh shall rest in hope: Because thou wilt not leave my soul in hell, neither wilt thou suffer thine Holy One to see corruption. Thou hast made known to me the ways of life; thou shalt make me full of joy with thy countenance* (Acts 2:25-28).

What is Peter doing here? He is using the Jewish Scriptures to build an ironclad case that Jesus is the long-awaited Messiah, David's descendant, but also David's Lord. And where is Jesus now? He was not just resurrected, but He was exalted and given the Holy Spirit to pour out upon all flesh—as they had just witnessed:

> *Therefore being by the right hand of God exalted, and having received of the Father the promise of the Holy Ghost, he hath shed forth this, which ye now see and hear* (Acts 2:33).

Hallelujah! Jesus' resurrection and exaltation guarantees YOUR resurrection!

THE CHURCH'S FIRST ALTAR CALL

Peter's Spirit-filled words produced just the results that Jesus had predicted:

> *And when he* [the Holy Spirit] *is come, he will reprove the world of sin, and of righteousness, and of judgment: Of sin, because they believe not on me; Of righteousness, because I go to my Father, and ye see me no more; Of judgment, because the prince of this world is judged* (John 16:8-11).

The multitude who stood before Peter was the same multitude who had cried, "Crucify Him; crucify Him," 50 days earlier. Now their actions must have flashed through their minds and brought with them a sense of sin and judgment. Guilt and remorse brought about the most important question a man can ask:

> *Now when they heard this, they were pricked in their heart, and said unto Peter and to the rest of the apostles, Men and brethren, what shall we do?* (Acts 2:37).

And Peter's answer to those sinners is the same answer for sinners today who want to be made right with God:

> *. . . Repent, and be baptized every one of you in the name of Jesus Christ for the remission of sins, and ye shall receive the gift of the Holy Ghost* (Acts 2:38).

Many among this crowd had no doubt heard John the Baptist preaching in the wilderness and baptizing those who wished to prepare their hearts for God's promised Messiah. This time the baptism would be in the name of Jesus; it would be a public acknowledgement that Jesus of Nazareth was both Messiah and Lord. Peter's preaching was obviously anointed:

> *Then they that gladly received his word were baptized: and the same day there were added unto them about three thousand souls* (Acts 2:41).

Isn't it just like God to reverse the curse that awaited those who had crucified His Son! Jesus had prayed, "Father, forgive them"; and Peter's sermon had been the vehicle used to bring forgiveness to the very ones who deserved eternal damnation. There is always an offer of mercy from God before a pronouncement of judgment. The Lord was calling *true Israel* out of physical Israel before the final cycle of discipline (mentioned in Leviticus 26) put an end to the dead, religious hypocrisy of Judaism that had turned its back on Israel's Savior. God's patience would wait 40 years before Jerusalem and its Temple would be burned to the ground and leveled by Roman soldiers in 70 A.D. God's true Temple would be the hearts of men and women who were filled with His Holy Spirit.

It was to the Jews first that the message of salvation was preached, and the believing remnant became charter members in the Church of Jesus Christ. According to Acts 2:42, four things marked this new group of people:

1. " . . . *they continued stedfastly in the apostles' doctrine . . . .*"

2. " . . . *they continued stedfastly in . . . fellowship, ...*"

3. " . . . *they continued stedfastly in . . . breaking of bread, ...*"

4. " . . . *they continued stedfastly in . . . prayers.*"

Anytime you have a group of Spirit-filled people who will give themselves to the teaching of the Word, fellowship, Communion, and prayers, they will have a noticeable effect upon those around them:

And fear came upon every soul: and many wonders and signs were done by the apostles (Acts 2:43).

COMMUNISM OR CHRISTIANITY?

The Bible does not teach communism. If believers are to have "all things common," it must be a work of the Holy Spirit—not the state. Nowhere in the New Testament are believers *commanded* to duplicate the Spirit's work during this special time of the Church's history. Remember that many of these new converts were from out-of-town; there was a genuine need for a sharing of food and lodging.

These first believers were Jews; consequently they met daily in the Temple area. What a time of joy and gladness— God was doing a new thing! Their oneness, singleness of heart, and spontaneous worship resulted in " . . . *favour with all the people.* . . . " (Acts 2:47). They had great miracles, great love, great unity, great joy—and great *growth:*

> . . . *And the Lord added to the church daily such as should be saved* (Acts 2:47).

If you and I will practice these same things *daily,* we will see the same results!

THE CHURCH'S FIRST MIRACLE OF HEALING

The acts of the Holy Spirit through the apostles, as we shall see, were miracles that set the stage for the preaching of the gospel. Chapter 3 of Acts is devoted to the first healing miracle performed by the Holy Spirit. Jesus had *begun* His ministry with a miracle at Cana of Galilee (John 2), and now we see Him *continue* that ministry through the apostle Peter.

It was the ninth hour, or three o'clock in the afternoon; Peter and John were still following the Jewish practice of praying toward or at the Temple three times a day. Solomon had begun the practice of praying toward Jerusalem:

> *If thy people go out to war against their enemies by the way that thou shalt send them, and they pray unto thee toward this city which thou hast chosen, and the house which I have built for thy name; Then hear thou from the heavens their prayer and their supplication, and maintain their cause* (II Chronicles 6:34,35).

King David prayed three times each day:

> *As for me, I will call upon God; and the LORD shall save me. Evening, and morning, and at noon, will I pray, and cry aloud: and he shall hear my voice* (Psalms 55:16,17).

Daniel followed this practice while he was captive in Babylon:

> *Now when Daniel knew that the writing was signed, he went into his house; and his windows being open in his chamber toward Jerusalem, he kneeled upon his knees three times a day, and prayed, and gave thanks before his God, as he did aforetime* (Daniel 6:10).

From the time they were little boys, Peter and John must have gone to the Temple thousands of times to pray. But this time would be different! This time they were filled with the Holy Spirit and empowered to continue the miracle-working ministry of Jesus. The story is a familiar one to many: a man born lame begged them for alms; and, although poor in material wealth, Peter was rich in spiritual power:

> *Then Peter said, Silver and gold have I none; but such as I have give I thee: In the name of Jesus Christ of Nazareth rise up and walk. And he took him by the right hand, and lifted him up: and immediately his feet and ankle bones received strength* (Acts 3:6,7).

This first miracle of healing in the Church did more than just heal a lame man. All Jerusalem must have passed this lame man at one time or another, and now the news of his miraculous healing spread quickly throughout the town. God was again drawing the net and preparing the way for another gospel message from Peter:

> *And as the lame man which was healed held Peter and John, all the people ran together unto them in the porch that is called Solomon's, greatly wondering. And when Peter saw it, he answered unto the people, Ye men of Israel, why marvel ye at this? or why look ye so earnestly on us, as though by our own power or holiness we had made this man to walk?* (Acts 3:11,12).

Peter's message came as the result of the miracle. Let's look at the points of his second sermon in Acts 3:12-26:

1. God has glorified Jesus through this miracle (vs. 12.13).

2. You killed God's Son, but God raised Him from the dead (vs. 14,15).

3. Faith in Jesus' name healed the lame man (v. 16).

4. Your actions were the result of ignorance; nevertheless, they were the fulfillment of prophecy (vs. 17,18).

5. Repent, and you will receive forgiveness (v. 19).

6. Jesus will return after God has restored all things spoken by the prophets (vs. 20,21).

7. Moses and all the prophets spoke of Jesus and of these days (vs. 22-25).

8. God sent Jesus to the Jews first to bless them with His forgiveness (v. 26).

THE CHURCH'S FIRST PERSECUTION

There are always two responses to the gospel: it is either received or rejected. Peter and John experienced both reactions; the Sadducees rejected the message. Why? They were "grieved" or *fed up* that Peter and John "... *preached through Jesus the resurrection from the dead"* (Acts 4:2). We know why that would be upsetting to them:

> *For the Sadducees say that there is no resurrection, neither angel, nor spirit: . . .* (Acts 23:8).

Peter's message ran contrary to the religious beliefs of these Jewish leaders. Unwilling to change their beliefs, they chose to attempt putting a stop to the message:

> *And they laid hands on them* [Peter and John], *and put them in hold unto the next day: for it was now eventide* (Acts 4:3).

But the Holy Spirit through Luke is also quick to point out the other response to Peter's message:

> *Howbeit many of them which heard the word believed; and the number of the men was about five thousand* (Acts 4:4).

TRIAL AND DEFENSE: PETER'S THIRD SERMON

The Jewish leaders couldn't argue about the miracle; too many people had seen the lame man at the gate, and now he was up and walking! Instead of denying the healing took place, they wanted to accuse Peter and John of using demonic powers:

*And when they had set them in the midst, they
asked, By what power, or by what name, have
ye done this?* (Acts 4:7).

What a loaded question! It was just what Peter (and the
Holy Spirit in Peter) needed to launch into another gospel
sermon! This time the message is short but powerful and
highly anointed:

*If we this day be examined of the good deed done
to the impotent man, by what means he is made
whole; Be it known unto you all, and to all the
people of Israel, that by the name of Jesus Christ
of Nazareth, whom ye crucified, whom God
raised from the dead, even by him doth this man
stand here before you whole. This is the stone
which was set at nought of you builders, which
is become the head of the corner. Neither is there
salvation in any other: for there is none other
name under heaven given among men, whereby
we must be saved* (Acts 4:9-12).

Can you believe that this is the same Peter speaking who
sheepishly denied Jesus when asked about Him by a young
woman? What boldness! Peter capitalized upon their
knowledge of the Scriptures to prick their hearts. He
referred to Jesus as the stone rejected by them:

*And he shall be for a sanctuary; but for a stone
of stumbling and for a rock of offence to both the
houses of Israel, for a gin and for a snare to
the inhabitants of Jerusalem* (Isaiah 8:14).

Jesus had earlier referred to Himself as the stone:

> *And have ye not read this scripture; The stone*
> *which the builders rejected is become the head*
> *of the corner* (Mark 12:10).

Peter leaves them hopeless with his last statement:

> *Neither is there salvation in any other: for there*
> *is none other name under heaven given among*
> *men, whereby we must be saved* (Acts 4:12).

"Sorry fellows," Peter says. "You've rejected your only hope of salvation. It's decision time for you! The fact that this lame man was made whole by the name and authority of Jesus proves that God raised Jesus from the dead and that God has put His stamp of approval upon Jesus' life and message."

The Jewish elders made their decision: they rejected Peter's sermon and tried to stop the *burning bush* that threatened to burn out of control if not stopped:

> *And they called them, and commanded them not*
> *to speak at all nor teach in the name of Jesus*
> (Acts 4:18).

Were these two fishermen intimidated by the Sanhedrin? Not at all! They went back to the growing group of believers and reported all that had been said and done, prayed for continued boldness and miracles, and received an immediate answer:

49

And when they had prayed, the place was shaken where they were assembled together; and they were all filled with the Holy Ghost, and they spake the word of God with boldness (Acts 4:31).

Notice the effect of persecution upon God's Church: rather than *restrict* the saints, it *released* the saints to speak the Word with boldness. Satan's outward attempt to douse the burning bush which was the Church had failed; but he didn't stop there. If *outward* persecution wouldn't work, there was always the possibility of corrupting the Church from *within*. But God's Church, as we shall see, met this challenge in the power of the Holy Spirit and grew all the stronger because of it!

CHAPTER THREE

Prison, Praise, & Persecution —the Church under Attack
(Acts 4:32-8:1)

The threats of the Jewish leaders failed to have any affect upon the growing Church. Intimidation is a powerless weapon against the genuine work of the Holy Spirit within a believer's heart. I remember reading the account of a group of Christians meeting in a Communist country. Their time of fellowship was interrupted by soldiers who broke up the meeting as they announced, "Anyone who wishes to renounce Jesus may leave; all others will be shot in five minutes!"

A few people did leave the building. After it was obvious that the others would not deny the name of Jesus, the guards locked the doors and said, "We are believers in Jesus, too, but we did not want to worship with anyone who was not totally committed to Christ. May we join your group?" Hallelujah! The presence of the Holy Spirit in a believer's life will result in boldness in the face of even death itself!

The first-century believers were living in the presence of the Holy Spirit—as evidenced by two things:

1. Their actions:

And the multitude of them that believed were of one heart and of one soul: neither said any of them that ought of the things which he possessed was his own; but they had all things common (Acts 4:32).

2. Their words:

And with great power gave the apostles witness of the resurrection of the Lord Jesus: and great grace was upon them all (Acts 4:33).

The Resurrection was the core of their preaching and teaching; without the truth of the Resurrection, Christianity is meaningless. Later, the apostle Paul would echo these same words as the gospel that he preached:

Moreover, brethren, I declare unto you the gospel which I preached unto you, which also ye have received, and wherein ye stand; By which also ye are saved, if ye keep in memory what I preached unto you, unless ye have believed in vain. For I delivered unto you first of all that which I also received, how that Christ died for our sins according to the scriptures; And that he was buried, and that he rose again the third day according to the scriptures (I Corinthians 15:1-4).

> *But if there be no resurrection of the dead, then*
> *is Christ not risen: And if Christ be not risen, then*
> *is our preaching vain, and your faith is also vain*
> (I Corinthians 15:13,14).

The "great power" with which the apostles preached the Resurrection resulted in "great grace" coming upon all the Church. It is the same today; those churches which experience great grace, great blessing, are the churches which preach a living, resurrected Christ.

BARNABAS— SON OF CONSOLATION

Luke introduces his readers to Barnabas, a believer who would eventually become a bridge for Paul to be introduced to the apostles in Jerusalem after his conversion. We're told that Barnabas, whose name means, "son of consolation," was a Levite, a priest whose relatives had evidently settled in Cyprus following the dispersion of the Jews to Assyria and Babylon. As a Levite, he was not to own property; but Luke tells us that Barnabas not only had land, but he also sold it and gave the money to the apostles. Barnabas, as we shall see, was a great *consolation* to the Church in more ways than one.

Barnabas would normally have taken at least a portion of his money to the Temple treasury. Now, however, the temple, or dwelling place of God, was the Church, Christ's Body:

What? know ye not that your body is the temple of the Holy Ghost which is in you, which ye have of God, and ye are not your own? (I Corinthians 6:19).

Those who sold their land or houses brought the proceeds (as much or as little as they felt led to give) as *freewill offerings* to the apostles for distribution to the needy. This was in accordance with Old Testament practice:

The children of Israel brought a willing offering unto the LORD, every man and woman, whose heart made them willing to bring for all manner of work, which the LORD had commanded to be made by the hand of Moses (Exodus 35:29).

For the poor shall never cease out of the land: therefore I command thee, saying, Thou shalt open thine hand wide unto thy brother, to thy poor, and to thy needy, in thy land (Deuteronomy 15:11).

God wants the same type of willingness and the same right attitude in giving from New Testament saints:

Every man according as he purposeth in his heart, so let him give; not grudgingly, or of necessity: for God loveth a cheerful giver (II Corinthians 9:7).

THE CHURCH'S FIRST SIN

Many people think that money is the root of all evil; the Bible doesn't say that! It is the *love* of money that is said to be the root of all evil (I Timothy 6:10). It is only when we divorce money from sense that sin deadens our conscience and dulls our spiritual lives.

It was not a sin for Ananias and Sapphira to own land, to sell it, nor to keep any or all of the money from the sale of that land. It is true that when God touches our hearts, He touches our checkbooks. The Lord had touched Barnabas' heart to give, and he gave out of love, not compulsion. Ananias and Sapphira, in contrast, gave out of greed—not for money, but for reputation. They lied about the *amount* given so that they would appear more generous than what was legitimately so. Theirs was the sin of hypocrisy which Jesus had denounced:

> *Woe unto you, scribes and Pharisees, hypocrites!*
> *for ye pay tithe of mint and anise and cummin,*
> *and have omitted the weightier matters of the*
> *law, judgment, mercy, and faith: these ought ye*
> *to have done, and not to leave the other undone*
> (Matthew 23:23).

There are five sins in the New Testament that are said to be sins against the Holy Spirit.

1. Resisting the Holy Spirit:

Ye stiffnecked and uncircumcised in heart and ears, ye do always resist the Holy Ghost: as your fathers did, so do ye (Acts 7:51).

2. Blasphemy against the Holy Spirit:

Wherefore I say unto you, All manner of sin and blasphemy shall be forgiven unto men: but the blasphemy against the Holy Ghost shall not be forgiven unto men (Matthew 12:31).

3. Grieving the Holy Spirit:

And grieve not the holy Spirit of God, whereby ye are sealed unto the day of redemption (Ephesians 4:30).

4. Quenching the Holy Spirit:

Quench not the Spirit (I Thessalonians 5:19).

5. Lying to the Holy Spirit:

But Peter said, Ananias, why hath Satan filled thine heart to lie to the Holy Ghost, and to keep back part of the price of the land? (Acts 5:3).

The result of this one lie was death. Peter was not the disciplinarian; the discipline came from God:

. . . thou hast not lied unto men, but unto God.

And Ananias hearing these words fell down, and gave up the ghost: . . . (Acts 5:4,5).

In His mercy, God does not immediately judge everyone who sins. The death of Ananias and Sapphira served as a warning to others in the early Church. Luke tells us twice the result of this Divine discipline:

. . . and great fear came on all them that heard these things (Acts 5:5).

And great fear came upon all the church, and upon as many as heard these things (Acts 5:11).

Fear can be a blessing:

The fear of the LORD *is the beginning of knowledge: . . .* (Proverbs 1:7).

THE CHURCH AND MIRACLES

After God's *purging* of the infant Church, Luke records the *power* of the Church:

And by the hands of the apostles were many signs and wonders wrought among the people; . . . Insomuch that they brought forth the sick into the streets, and laid them on beds and couches, that at the least the shadow of Peter

*passing by might overshadow some of them.
There came also a multitude out of the cities
round about unto Jerusalem, bringing sick
folks, and them which were vexed with unclean
spirits: and they were healed every one*
(Acts 5:12,15,16).

Here we read a description of the Church continuing the
works which "Jesus began to do" (Acts 1:1). Luke used
similar words to describe the ministry of Jesus:

*And he [Jesus] came down with them, and stood
in the plain, and the company of his disciples,
and a great multitude of people out of all Judea
and Jerusalem, and from the sea coast of Tyre
and Sidon, which came to hear him, and to be
healed of their diseases; And they that were
vexed with unclean spirits: and they were
healed. And the whole multitude sought to touch
him: for there went virtue out of him, and healed
them all* (Luke 6:17-19).

The healings mentioned in Luke 6 were only the
beginning of what Jesus came to do; now He was
continuing those works through His Body. Jesus had
appealed to His works to validate His message:

*If I do not the works of my Father, believe me
not. But if I do, though ye believe not me, believe
the works: that ye may know, and believe, that
the Father is in me, and I in him* (John 10:37,38).

Now the Church was performing the same works as a sign to validate the gospel message of Jesus' life, death, and resurrection. Later the apostle Paul would write, *"For the Jews require a sign, . . . "* (I Corinthians 1:22). God gave them "signs and wonders" to turn their hearts toward the forgiveness and new life He offered to all; multitudes saw the signs and believed the message—but not everyone believed. Whenever there are great miracles, there seems to be great persecution. God's burning bush, the Church, was shining brighter and brighter—which no doubt infuriated Satan!

GREATER PERSECUTION

As God added daily to His Church through the preaching of the apostles, the high priest, along with the Sadducees, sought for a way to put an end to the apostles' teaching about the Resurrection:

> *Then the high priest rose up, and all they that were with him, (which is the sect of the Sadducees,) and were filled with indignation, And laid their hands on the apostles, and put them in the common prison* (Acts 5:17,18).

The prison hasn't been built that can hold God's people when He wants them free. The Lord sent an angel to release the apostles and to show the Sanhedrin that they were fighting a losing battle against God. The angel gave instructions for the apostles to return to the Temple area and speak *" . . . all the words of this life"* (Acts 5:20).

The apostles obeyed, while at the same time the religious leaders sent guards to the prison to bring the prisoners before the council again. Imagine their frustration when the guards returned with this unsettling news:

> . . . *The prison truly found we shut with all safety, and the keepers standing without before the doors: but when we had opened, we found no man within* (Acts 5:23).

That was strange indeed; but what no doubt perplexed them even more was the news that their prisoners had gone right back to teaching the people in the Temple area! This time the captain of the guards went with his men to arrest the apostles for the third time. The high priest presented the charges against these emboldened men:

> . . . *Did not we straitly command you that ye should not teach in this name? and, behold, ye have filled Jerusalem with your doctrine, and intend to bring this man's blood upon us* (Acts 5:28).

It was the chief priests who had persuaded the multitude to ask for the release of Barabbas so that Jesus would be crucified, and they were among the crowd who had said to Pilate, " . . . *His blood be on us, and on our children*" (Matthew 27:25). The apostles had not brought Jesus' blood upon the chief priests; they brought it upon themselves!

Peter and the apostles didn't have to search for words in answering the high priest:

> . . . *We ought to obey God rather than men* (Acts 5:29).

Peter went on to remind the council that they killed God's Messiah, but God raised Him from the dead and exalted Him to be the Savior of Israel. Repentance and forgiveness of sins was now being offered to all of Israel. Peter's defense brought an immediate response:

> *When they heard that, they were cut to the heart, and took counsel to slay them* (Acts 5:33).

Earlier a crowd had heard Peter preach, and the response was quite different:

> *Now when they heard this, they were pricked in their heart, and said unto Peter and to the rest of the apostles, Men and brethren, what shall we do?* (Acts 2:37).

The result was 3,000 souls saved through repentance leading to the new birth. Although the religious leaders heard the same message, they hardened their hearts even more and sought for a way to kill the apostles *and* their gospel.

Notice what happened next: a *Pharisee* on the council stood up and gave his peers a warning. Remember, this man believed in a resurrection so he was more sympathetic toward the teaching of Peter and the other apostles. His name was Gamaliel; he was a major religious leader and teacher. One of his students was none other than Saul (Paul) of Tarsus:

> *I* [Paul] *am verily a man which am a Jew, born in Tarsus, a city in Cilicia, yet brought up on this city at the feet of Gamaliel, and taught according to the perfect manner of the law of the fathers, and was zealous toward God, as ye all are this day* (Acts 22:3).

Gamaliel gave the council some excellent advice:

> . . . *Refrain from these men, and let them alone: for if this counsel or this work be of men, it will come to nought: But if it be of God, ye cannot overthrow it; lest haply ye be found even to fight against God* (Acts 5:38,39).

The Sadducees and the high priest so respected Gamaliel that they took his advice. Nevertheless, the apostles were beaten, commanded not to speak about Jesus again, and released. Rather than complain about their flogging for the name of Jesus, the disciples were ". . . *rejoicing that they were counted worthy to suffer shame for his name*" (Acts 5:41).

Despite greater persecution the Church continued to grow. The apostles were not deterred by internal or external pressures. Luke tells us about the activities of these Church fathers:

*And daily in the temple, and in every house,
they ceased not to teach and preach Jesus Christ*
(Acts 5:42).

THE CHURCH'S FIRST STRIFE

Chapter 6 verse 1 contains the three "m's":

The disciples **multiplied.**

The Grecians **murmured.**

The strife was over the daily **ministration.**

Nothing can cause the split of a church faster than strife amongst its members. The problem here in the book of Acts was between those Jews of the dispersion who spoke the Greek language of their homelands and the Hebrew-speaking Jews who lived in Israel. The Grecian Jews felt that their widows were being shortchanged when provisions were distributed (see Acts 2:44,45).

I love how the apostles resolved this potentially church-splitting issue:

*Then the twelve called the multitude of the
disciples unto them, and said, . . . Wherefore,
brethren, look ye out among you seven . . .*
(Acts 6:2,3).

63

The "multitude" were told to find certain men with the qualifications to handle the situation:

> . . . *men of honest report, full of the Holy Ghost and wisdom,* . . . (Acts 6:3).

It was the apostles' decision to delegate the work of serving tables, but the multitude was given the task of finding the right men to do the job. Once the right men were found, the apostles ordained them through the laying on of hands:

> *And the saying pleased the whole multitude: and they chose Stephen, a man full of faith and of the Holy Ghost, and Philip, and Prochorus, and Nicanor, and Timon, and Parmenas, and Nicolas a proselyte of Antioch: Whom they set before the apostles: and when they had prayed, they laid their hands on them* (Acts 6:5,6).

These men were the first deacons of the Church. *Deacon* comes from the Greek word *diakonia,* which means "hand." A deacon, then, is someone who lends a hand where help is needed.

The Church had survived another attempt to put out its flaming testimony, and the result was a brighter fire:

> *And the word of God increased; and the number of the disciples multiplied in Jerusalem greatly; . . . And Stephen, full of faith and power, did*

great wonders and miracles among the people
(Acts 6:7,8).

Opposition only serves to make the Church stronger!
God, by His Spirit in men, is able to overcome every
obstacle or roadblock that Satan tries to erect against the
Lord's burning bush; this gospel flame is eternal! Notice
that by now even the *priests* were being swept along in
this Holy Ghost revival:

> *. . . and a great company of the priests were
> obedient to the faith* (Acts 6:7).

THE CHURCH'S FIRST MARTYR: STEPHEN

It was now the *unbelievers* turn to murmur! Stephen's
great wonders and miracles brought on great opposition
from a number of groups:

> *Then there arose certain of the synagogue, which
> is called the synagogue of the Libertines, and
> Cyrenians, and Alexandrians, and of them of
> Cilicia and of Asia, disputing with Stephen*
> (Acts 6:9).

Here we read about five groups of Jews ganging up on
one Spirit-filled layman in the Church. I feel sorry (almost)
for the Jews, because the odds were definitely stacked
against them!

The first group were from the synagogue of the Libertines. These were either freed Jews who left Rome when Tiberius expelled all Jews from the city around 20 A.D. or perhaps they were from the city of Libertina, Africa.

When the Jews were held in Assyrian and Babylonian captivity, they congregated to hear the Old Testament read and explained by their priests. Each city or area had its own synagogue as a center of worship while the Jews were away from the Temple in Jerusalem. After the dispersion synagogues arose in Israel and were attended by groups who had returned together and knew each other from the days of the captivity.

Other men from the areas of Cyrene and Alexandria, Africa, and the areas of Cilicia and Asia, came together to argue with Stephen. Those from Cilicia no doubt were from the same synagogue in which Paul grew up. Despite the best teaching and training these men had in their religious centers throughout the world, they were no match for Stephen:

> And they were not able to resist the wisdom and the spirit by which he [Stephen] spake (Acts 6:10).

When these men couldn't win their argument legally, they resorted to illegal means by putting forth some men who lied about Stephen:

> Then they suborned men, which said, We have

heard him speak blasphemous words against
Moses, and against God (Acts 6:11).

Once again opposition to what God was doing through His Church set up the perfect situation for the preaching of the gospel to the Sanhedrin. Notice God's goodness in sharing the message of repentance and forgiveness so many times with these religious leaders!

STEPHEN'S DEFENSE

When the high priest asked Stephen, "Are these things so?" it was just the opportunity he was looking for to launch into a Spirit-led sermon, which included a marvelous review of Israel's history, beginning with God's appearance to Abraham. Stephen really knew the Word of God! You and I need to know the Word of God like Stephen so that we can be used of the Holy Spirit when an occasion arises that requires us to speak.

Stephen presented Israel's history down to the time of Solomon's Temple. BUT, he concluded to these priests who were so proud of their magnificent Temple, God doesn't dwell in man-made buildings. A quote from Isaiah capped his argument:

Heaven is my throne, and earth is my footstool:
what house will ye build me? saith the Lord: or
what is the place of my rest? Hath not my hand
made all these things? (Acts 7:49,50).

If that wasn't enough to set the religious leaders back a bit, Stephen personalized his message even more by boldly accusing the Sanhedrin of rebellion and murder:

> *Ye stiffnecked and uncircumcised in heart and ears, ye do always resist the Holy Ghost: as your fathers did, so do ye. Which of the prophets have not your fathers persecuted? and they have slain them which shewed before of the coming of the Just One; of whom ye have been now the betrayers and murderers: Who have received the law by the disposition of angels, and have not kept it* (Acts 7:51-53).

Let's look at the charges Stephen made against these men, and maybe we'll understand God's indignation at the Jewish nation as a whole when it rejected His Savior:

1. They were stiffnecked (v. 51).

2. They were uncircumcised in heart (v. 51).

3. They were uncircumcised in ears (v. 51).

4. They were resisting the Holy Spirit (v. 51).

5. They betrayed their Messiah (v. 52).

6. They murdered their Messiah (v. 52).

7. They broke the law (v. 53).

Once again they had the option of accepting or rejecting the truth; they chose to reject it:

> *When they heard these things, they were cut to the heart, and they gnashed on him with their teeth* (Acts 7:54).

God had the most wonderful way of keeping Stephen calm, cool, and collected; He drew heaven's curtain aside so that Stephen could have a glimpse of glory:

> *But he* [Stephen], *being full of the Holy Ghost, looked up stedfastly into heaven, and saw the glory of God, and Jesus standing on the right hand of God. And said, Behold, I see the heavens opened, and the Son of man standing on the right hand of God* (Acts 7:55,56).

Why do you suppose that Jesus was *standing* at the Father's right hand? Everywhere else in the New Testament we read that Jesus is *seated* at the right hand of God. I believe Jesus stood in anticipation of receiving the first Christian martyr:

> *Then they cried out with a loud voice, and stopped their ears, and ran upon him with one accord, And cast him out of the city, and stoned him:* . . . (Acts 7:57,58).

Before they picked up the boulders to throw at Stephen, the Sanhedrin laid their coats at the feet of Saul. Stephen's defense and composure at his stoning no doubt had a tremendous impact upon Saul. I don't believe that Stephen felt any pain. It was Stephen's prayer just before his death that God answered in transforming the Christian-hater, Saul, into the giant apostle of the faith, Paul:

And they stoned Stephen, calling upon God, and saying, Lord Jesus, receive my spirit. And he kneeled down, and cried with a loud voice, Lord, lay not this sin to their charge. And when he had said this, he fell asleep (Acts 7:59,60).

Forgiveness on our part is so important if we are to see others come into the kingdom of God. Satan was so enraged at Stephen's behavior that he caused the persecution to spread throughout the Church. In the next chapter we shall see that when the Church was scattered through persecution, the result backfired on the devil; and the burning bush that glowed so brightly in Jerusalem was flung in all directions in fulfilment of Jesus' command to take the gospel to Samaria!

CHAPTER FOUR

God Gets His Man
—Saul Meets the Risen Lord
(Acts 8:2-9:31)

The persecution that Satan thought would eliminate the Church was the very thing that God used to spread the gospel into new areas. When Saul's persecution of the believers began, we can see the second stage in the development of the Church. Up until this time, the major ministry had been under the apostles in Jerusalem. Now, the action shifted over to Philip, which shows that it takes all the members—not just the apostles—to fulfill the Great Commission. The persecution scattered the Church, but it didn't cause it to wither and die. The Church grew from Jerusalem, to Judea, to Samaria, to Asia, and to Rome. It's like kicking the embers of a fire—it scatters them, but it doesn't put them out!

Saul made "havoc" of the Church; he was like an animal seeking its prey. Paul confessed to putting the Christians into prison and testifying against them before their deaths:

*Which thing I also did in Jerusalem: and many
of the saints did I shut up in prison, having
received authority from the chief priests; and
when they were put to death, I gave my voice
against them* (Acts 26:10).

Later Paul would write that he acted out of ignorance:

*Who was before a blasphemer, and a persecutor,
and injurious: but I obtained mercy, because I did
it ignorantly in unbelief* (I Timothy 1:13).

SAMARIA HEARS THE GOSPEL

As a result of the persecution, Philip, one of the deacons
chosen earlier, traveled to the region of Samaria:

*Then Philip went down to the city of Samaria,
and preached Christ unto them* (Acts 8:5).

See map on page 216.

Samaria was a hated place by the Jews; when the people
of the northern kingdom were taken captive to Assyria, the
king of Assyria replaced them with pagans from different
countries:

*And the king of Assyria brought men from
Babylon, and from Cuthah, and from Ava, and*

*from Hamath, and from Sepharvaim, and placed
them in the cities of Samaria instead of the
children of Israel: and they possessed Samaria,
and dwelt in the cities thereof. And so it was at
the beginning of their dwelling there, that they
feared not the LORD: . . .* (II Kings 17:24,25).

When the Jews came back from the Babylonian captivity,
many of them divorced their wives to marry Samaritan
women. As a result, they were not allowed to worship in
the Temple at Jerusalem. That didn't bother them—they
built their own "Temple" on Mt. Gerizim and started their
own form of Judaism!

Several years ago, I had the opportunity to visit what is
now called the "Temple of the Samaritans," which is in
Nabulus, an Arab city. It certainly is far from being a temple;
it is more like a little house-church. There is a very small
number of Samaritans who attend, and many of them
have birth defects because they have intermarried. It is
rather tragic.

Thus the Samaritans were despised by the Jews—but not
by God. Jesus had purposely gone through Samaria, talked
to a woman there, and predicted a great harvest to come
out of that city:

*Say not ye, There are yet four months, and then
cometh harvest? behold, I say unto you, Lift up
your eyes, and look on the fields; for they are
white already to harvest* (John 4:35).

The persecution of the Church and Philip's trip to Samaria were both part of the fulfillment of the harvest that Jesus saw in that town. Philip "preached Christ" to the people, performed miracles, and revival hit:

> *And the people with one accord gave heed unto those things which Philip spake, hearing and seeing the miracles which he did. And there was great joy in that city* (Acts 8:6,8).

In contrast to the power of God flowing through Philip, we read about one Simon the sorcerer. It seems that the townspeople attributed great supernatural powers to Simon. But Simon and his tricks were no match for Philip's preaching of the kingdom of God and the name of Jesus:

> *But when they believed Philip preaching the things concerning the kingdom of God, and the name of Jesus Christ, they were baptized, both men and women* (Acts 8:12).

Luke tells us that even Simon believed and was baptized; however, I do not believe he was truly regenerated. As we shall see, his motive for "believing" was purely self-centered. He simply was amazed by the miracle-working power demonstrated by Philip:

> *Then Simon himself believed also: and when he was baptized, he continued with Philip, and wondered, beholding the miracles and signs which were done* (Acts 8:13).

The revival at Samaria was such that news of it reached all the way back to Jerusalem! The apostles decided to send Peter and John down to investigate. This was the same John who had previously asked Jesus to send fire down on the Samaritans:

> *And when his disciples James and John saw this, they said, Lord, wilt thou that we command fire to come down from heaven, and consume them, even as Elias did?* (Luke 9:54).

Now John would be used of God to bring the fire of the Holy Spirit baptism to these same people:

> *Who, when they were come down, prayed for them, that they might receive the Holy Ghost: Then laid they their hands on them, and they received the Holy Ghost* (Acts 8:15,17).

Now we see a confrontation between the two Simons: Simon the sorcerer and Simon Peter:

> *And when Simon saw that through laying on of the apostles' hands the Holy Ghost was given, he offered them money, But Peter said unto him, Thy money perish with thee, because thou hast thought that the gift of God may be purchased with money* (Acts 8:18,20).

Peter told Simon to repent, but there doesn't seem to have been any real heartfelt repentance. Simon was more concerned over the *consequences* of his actions than anything else.

On their way back to Jerusalem, Peter and John preached the gospel in many villages of the Samaritans. True conversion will work a miracle in a person's heart attitudes. Peter and John were displaying the fruit of the Holy Spirit in their lives and making their enemies be at peace with them:

> *When a man's ways please the LORD, he maketh even his enemies to be at peace with him* (Proverbs 16:7).

At this point in the book of Acts, three parts of Jesus' command in Acts 1:8 had been fulfilled: the gospel had been preached in Jerusalem, Judea, and Samaria. The Holy Spirit was now ready to spread God's burning bush into the uttermost parts of the earth.

Have you noticed how God is breaking down the wall of separation between all races and types of peoples? Here in chapter 8 we will see the conversion of the Ethiopian eunuch, a black man from the family of Ham. In chapter 9 Paul, a Jew from the family of Shem, will become a member of Christ's Body. And in chapter 10 Cornelius, a Roman from the racial family of Japheth, will receive the Holy Spirit. The Church is the one place where all men are made one:

> *But now in Christ Jesus ye who sometimes were far off are made nigh by the blood of Christ. For he is our peace, who hath made both one, and hath*

broken down the middle wall of partition between us (Ephesians 2:13,14).

A GENTILE HEARS THE GOSPEL

Philip had just finished preaching to the lowly, hated Samaritans. They had given attention to his message because of the miracles of healing and exorcism performed in their midst. Philip's next assignment from the Holy Spirit would be quite different. This time he was sent to a spiritually hungry officer of Ethiopia (see map on page 216) who needed only to hear Philip's explanation of the Word of God in order to believe the good news about Jesus:

> *And the eunuch answered Philip, and said, I pray thee, of whom speaketh the prophet this? of himself, or of some other man? Then Philip opened his mouth, and began at the same scripture, and preached unto him Jesus* (Acts 8:34,35).

The scripture in question was a portion of Isaiah. Philip was holding his first Bible Encounter and beholding Jesus in the book of Isaiah! As Christians, we need to be able to find and to preach Jesus from every book of the Bible. Philip's sharing resulted in the first gentile salvation:

> *And Philip said, If thou believest with all thine heart, thou mayest. And he answered and said, I believe that Jesus Christ is the Son of God* (Acts 8:37).

Following his conversion, the eunuch was baptized and ". . . *went on his way rejoicing*" (Acts 8:39). The gospel brings joy wherever it goes!

SAUL MEETS THE RISEN LORD

The persecution that scattered the Christians living in Jerusalem no doubt led some to seek refuge in Damascus. Saul was determined to bring them back to Jerusalem for trial:

> *And desired of him letters to Damascus to the synagogues, that if he found any of this way, whether they were men or women, he might bring them bound unto Jerusalem* (Acts 9:2).

But the one who tried to arrest the believers was arrested himself as he traveled, "breathing out threatenings and slaughter," on the road to Damascus. "High noon" for Saul was the time for his encounter with the One Whom he would call, "the Lord from heaven":

> *And it came to pass, that, as I made my journey, and was come nigh unto Damascus about noon, suddenly there shone from heaven a great light round about me* (Acts 22:6).

> *At midday, O king, I saw in the way a light from heaven, above the brightness of the sun, shining*

*round about me and them which journeyed with
me* (Acts 26:13).

*The first man is of the earth, earthy: the second
man is the Lord from heaven* (I Corinthians 15:47).

See map on page 217.

The Lord's question to Saul shows the vital link between
Jesus and His mystical Body of believers:

*And he [Saul] fell to the earth, and heard a voice
saying unto him, Saul, Saul, why persecutest thou
me? And he said, Who art thou, Lord? And the
Lord said, I am Jesus whom thou persecutest: it
is hard for thee to kick against the pricks*
(Acts 9:4,5).

What were the "pricks" that Saul had kicked against?
Undoubtedly the words of Stephen as he died stayed in
Saul's memory to haunt him; and the love, zeal, and courage
of the Christians he had sentenced to death never left his
mind. Again and again God dealt with Saul through
believers, but he continued to ignore the Lord.

Saul "... *trembling and astonished said, Lord, what wilt
thou have me to do? ...* "(Acts 9:6). Saul called Him "Lord,"
and from that time forward, Jesus would be Lord in Saul's
heart, mind, soul, and will. That day the old Saul died with
Christ, and the new Saul stood forth. He would exalt Jesus
perhaps as no other man. Saul was blinded physically, but
he saw everything clearly with his spirit. The men with him

could see with the human eye, but they really saw nothing because they failed to see Jesus.

Have you ever been to a harbor and watched the little tug boats as they guide the huge ocean liners in and out of port? Luke introduces us now to one of God's "tugboats," who was used to launch the giant apostle of the faith into his ministry. Ananias, an unknown believer living in the city of Damascus, was obedient to the Lord's instructions:

> *And Ananias went his way, and entered into the house; and putting his hands on him said, Brother Saul, the Lord, even Jesus, that appeared unto thee in the way as thou camest, hath sent me, that thou mightest receive thy sight, and be filled with the Holy Ghost* (Acts 9:17).

Notice that Saul was already a "brother." The Lord, however, chose to use a faithful new convert like Ananias to impart the baptism of the Holy Spirit to Saul.

Although he had not eaten nor drank anything for three days, Saul's first request was to be baptized. He no doubt had seen and heard of this Christian practice that meant so much to believers. Any Jew who was publicly baptized was immediately cut off from his or her family. The new Christian was officially considered dead by parents and relatives. Saul lost one family but gained a much larger and eternal one.

Now years and years of Old Testament study would finally come alive for Saul. All the prophecies concerning the coming of Messiah, His miracles, His rejection, His death, and His resurrection, suddenly had meaning. Saul lost no time in sharing his fresh revelation of Christ in the Scriptures with the Jews at Damascus:

> *And straightway he preached Christ in the synagogues, that he is the Son of God. But Saul increased the more in strength, and confounded the Jews which dwelt at Damascus, proving that this is very Christ* (Acts 9:20,22).

Saul's preaching was not well received by some; they took council to kill him! Between his escape from Damascus (Acts 9:25) and his visit to Jerusalem (Acts 9:26), Saul spent three years praying and meditating before the Lord:

> *Then after three years I went up to Jerusalem to see Peter, and abode with him fifteen days* (Galatians 1:18).

The Lord used another *middle man*, this time Barnabas, to further the work that He wanted to do through Saul:

> *And when Saul was come to Jerusalem, he assayed to join himself to the disciples: but they were all afraid of him, and believed not that he was a disciple. But Barnabas took him, and brought him to the apostles, and declared unto them how he had seen the Lord in the way, and that he had spoken to him, and how he had preached boldly at Damascus in the name of Jesus* (Acts 9:26,27).

Because of another attempt on Saul's life at Jerusalem, the Christians there sent him away to his hometown of Tarsus:

> *And he spake boldly in the name of the Lord Jesus, and disputed against the Grecians: but they went about to slay him. Which when the brethren knew, they brought him down to Caesarea, and sent him forth to Tarsus* (Acts 9:29,30).

This is the last we read of Saul until Acts 11:30, nearly ten years later! No doubt Saul went to the synagogues there to confront the Jews with the good news of Jesus Christ, their Messiah. Meanwhile, the Holy Spirit was using the apostle Peter to perform miracles and to open the door of salvation to a God-fearing gentile named Cornelius.

CHAPTER FIVE

The Gentiles Get the Message—Eleven Years Later
(Acts 9:32-12:25)

Today, many in the Church of Jesus Christ would try to tell us that miracles have ceased: "Miracles were for the early Church," these people argue. But don't you believe it! As we shall see, miracles were used by the Lord to expand the first-century Church, which raises the question, "Does the twentieth-century Church need to expand?" Yes! God's true Church will always operate in the supernatural in fulfilling the Great Commission of making disciples of all nations:

> Go ye therefore, and teach all nations, baptizing them in the name of the Father, and of the Son, and of the Holy Ghost: Teaching them to observe all things whatsoever I have commanded you: and, lo, I am with you alway, even unto the end of the world. Amen (Matthew 28:19,20).

ACTS

Fortunately, the Holy Spirit, through Luke, is careful to tell us not only *what* happened at the hands of the apostles, but also the *results* of what happened. The story of Peter's healing of a paralyzed man is a case in point. Luke tells us that Peter said, "*. . . Jesus Christ maketh thee whole: arise, and make thy bed. . . .*" (Acts 9:34). The man "arose immediately." That's *what* happened; now notice the *result*:

> *And all that dwelt at Lydda and Saron saw him, and turned to the Lord* (Acts 9:35).

Hallelujah! The miracle turned a whole region around! (See map page 218.) Miracles are not for miracles' sake; they are to turn people to the Lord. News of Peter's visit to Lydda spread to Joppa where the Lord was about to perform an even greater miracle through Peter—the resurrection of Dorcas:

> *Now there was at Joppa a certain disciple named Tabitha, which by interpretation is called Dorcas: this woman was full of good works and almsdeeds which she did. And it came to pass in those days, that she was sick, and died: whom when they had washed, they laid her in an upper chamber* (Acts 9:36,37).

Dorcas wouldn't lie there for long; the disciples in Joppa sent for Peter. After walking the ten miles from Lydda to Joppa, Peter "*. . . kneeled down, and prayed; and turning him to the body said, Tabitha, arise. And she opened her eyes: and when she saw Peter, she sat up*" (Acts 9:40).

Another miracle! And Luke doesn't neglect to tell us the *result* of this miracle:

> *And it was known throughout all Joppa; and many believed in the Lord. And it came to pass, that he [Peter] tarried many days in Joppa with one Simon a tanner* (Acts 9:42,43).

It was the miraculous that caused many to believe in the Lord. Peter no doubt took the opportunity to solidify the new converts' faith by teaching them the Old Testament's prophecies about the Messiah. The "many days" he spent in Joppa could have been as long as three years—just as it was in the case of Shimei in the days of Solomon:

> *. . . And Shimei dwelt in Jerusalem many days. And it came to pass at the end of three years, that two of the servants of Shimei ran away . . .* (I Kings 2:38,39).

At any rate Peter's stay in Joppa was with a tanner. This interesting fact reveals the breakdown of Peter's strict Jewish upbringing; anyone who handled the hides of clean or unclean animals was looked down upon by the Jews. If a woman was betrothed to a man and she found he was a tanner, she could break her betrothal. The Lord was certainly getting Peter ready for the gentile Pentecost (in Acts chapter 10) at the house of Cornelius!

GENTILE SALVATION

During the ministry of Jesus on the earth, the disciples
were told to take their message only to the Jews:

> *These twelve Jesus sent forth, and commanded
> them, saying, Go not into the way of the Gentiles,
> and into any city of the Samaritans enter ye not:
> But go rather to the lost sheep of the house of
> Israel* (Matthew 10:5,6).

Because the Jews rejected their Messiah, the way was
opened for the gentiles to participate in God's kingdom:

> *Therefore say I* [Jesus] *unto you, The kingdom of
> God shall be taken from you* [Jews], *and given
> to a nation bringing forth the fruits thereof*
> (Matthew 21:43).

The Messiah's rejection had not taken God by surprise;
the gentiles were prophesied to be a part of God's
blessings all along:

> *And in that day there shall be a root of Jesse,
> which shall stand for an ensign of the people; to
> it shall the Gentiles seek: and his rest shall be
> glorious* (Isaiah 11:10).

> *I the* LORD *have called thee in righteousness, and
> will hold thine hand, and will keep thee, and give
> thee for a covenant of the people, for a light of the*

Gentiles; To open the blind eyes, to bring out the prisoners from the prison, and them that sit in darkness out of the prison house (Isaiah 42:6,7).

And he said, It is a light thing that thou shouldest be my servant to raise up the tribes of Jacob, and to restore the preserved of Israel: I will also give thee for a light to the Gentiles, that thou mayest be my salvation unto the end of the earth (Isaiah 49:6).

For thou shalt break forth on the right hand and on the left; and thy seed shall inherit the Gentiles, and make the desolate cities to be inhabited (Isaiah 54:3).

Therefore thy gates shall be open continually; they shall not be shut day nor night; that men may bring unto thee the forces of the Gentiles, and that their kings may be brought (Isaiah 60:11).

And I will set a sign among them, and I will send those that escape of them unto the nations, to Tarshish, Pul, and Lud, that draw the bow, to Tubal, and Javan, to the isles afar off, that have not heard my fame, neither have seen my glory; and they shall declare my glory among the Gentiles (Isaiah 66:19).

O LORD, my strength, and my fortress, and my refuge in the day of affliction, the Gentiles shall come unto thee from the ends of the earth, and

*shall say, Surely our fathers have inherited lies,
vanity, and things wherein there is no profit*
(Jeremiah 16:19).

*For from the rising of the sun even unto the going
down of the same my name shall be great among
the Gentiles; and in every place incense shall be
offered unto my name, and a pure offering: for
my name shall be great among the heathen, saith
the LORD of hosts* (Malachi 1:11).

*And the scripture, foreseeing that God would
justify the heathen through faith, preached before
the gospel unto Abraham, saying, In thee shall all
nations be blessed. . . . That the blessing of
Abraham might come on the Gentiles through
Jesus Christ; that we might receive the promise
of the Spirit through faith* (Galatians 3:8,14).

For its first 11 years, or so, the Church was composed
almost exclusively of Jews. Let's take a close look at the
chronology of the book of Acts:

ACTS TIME LINE

EVENT	REFERENCE	APPROXIMATE DATE A.D.	# OF YEARS AFTER ASCENSION
Ascension	Acts 1	30	0
Pentecost	Acts 2	30	0
Stephen stoned	Acts 6,7	35	5
Paul converted	Acts 9	35	5
Cornelius saved	Acts 10	41	11
Saul & Barnabas in Antioch	Acts 11	43	13
James killed	Acts 12	44	14
Paul's 1st trip Wrote Galatians (?)*	Acts 13	45	15
Jerusalem Council	Acts 15	50	20
Paul's 2nd trip Stayed at Corinth 1½ years; Wrote I,II Thess., Galatians (?)*	Acts 15	50	20
Paul's 3rd trip At Ephesus wrote I,II Corinthians	Acts 18	54	24
At Corinth wrote Romans			
Paul's arrest and trials	Acts 21	58	28
Paul sent to Rome (1st imprisonment) Wrote Col., Philem., Eph., Phil.	Acts 27	60 61-63	30
While free, wrote I Tim., Titus, Hebrews (?)			
(2nd imprisonment) Wrote II Timothy		67	37
Paul's death		67	37

*There is disagreement among Bible scholars as to when Paul wrote Galatians. Both Paul's letter to the Galatians and the Jerusalem Council dealt with the fundamental issue of legalism, and *both* came to the same conclusion: Salvation is by faith alone.

In God's timing, the door was now to be opened to the gentiles to have equal footing with the Jews in Christ's Church. It would take something spectacular to convince the Jews of God's equal treatment—totally apart from the law and Jewish traditions—of the gentiles. The Ethiopian eunuch was an isolated gentile who most likely was already a Jewish proselyte before his conversion (see Acts 8:26-28). Peter was the perfect choice to witness the outpouring of the Holy Spirit on the gentiles, and Cornelius and his household were God's chosen recipients of that gift.

Cornelius lived in Caesarea, which was a gentile city and the seat of Roman power in Israel. It lies 55 miles north of Jerusalem, but on the coast, about one day's journey from Joppa. (See map page 218.)

God sent an angel to Cornelius while he was praying at the time of the evening sacrifice. If you've ever wanted to build a memorial, take note of the angel's message:

> . . . *Thy prayers and thine alms are come up for a memorial before God* (Acts 10:4).

Lasting, *eternal* memorials, are built on prayer and deeds of love to those around us. Cornelius was a devout man who put himself in a place where he could hear from God. It is not enough, however, just to *hear* from God—notice that Cornelius was *obedient* to what God told him to do:

> *And now send men to Joppa, and call for one Simon, whose surname is Peter: He lodgeth with one Simon a tanner, whose house is by the sea*

side: he shall tell thee what thou oughtest to do (Acts 10:5,6).

The day after God spoke to Cornelius, He prepared Peter for gentile visitors:

On the morrow, as they went on their journey, and drew nigh unto the city, Peter went up upon the housetop to pray about the sixth hour: And he became very hungry, and would have eaten: but while they made ready, he fell into a trance (Acts 10:9,10).

Peter saw a sheet filled with unclean animals descending before him, and a voice told him to "kill and eat." Imagine Peter's horror at the prospect of eating animals forbidden by the Mosaic dietary laws! Peter's response was, " . . . *Not so, Lord; for I have never eaten any thing that is common or unclean*" (Acts 10:14). The voice told Peter, " . . . *What God hath cleansed, that call not thou common*" (Acts 10:15).

The vision was repeated *three times* to establish it firmly into Peter's thinking:

One witness shall not rise up against a man for any iniquity, or for any sin, in any sin that he sinneth: at the mouth of two witnesses, or at the mouth of three witnesses, shall the matter be established (Deuteronomy 19:15).

This is the third time I am coming to you. In the mouth of two or three witnesses shall every word be established (II Corinthians 13:1).

The gentiles were considered "common or unclean" by the Jews, and the gentile nations were often symbolized by animals in the Bible:

> *Daniel spake and said, I saw in my vision by night, and, behold, the four winds of the heaven strove upon the great sea. And four great beasts came up from the sea, diverse one from another* (Daniel 7:2,3).

> *Then I lifted up mine eyes, and saw, and, behold, there stood before the river a ram which had two horns: . . . And as I was considering, behold, an he goat came from the west on the face of the whole earth, . . .* (Daniel 8:3,5).

> *And the beast which I saw was like unto a leopard, and his feet were as the feet of a bear, and his mouth as the mouth of a lion: and the dragon gave him his power, and his seat, and great authority* (Revelation 13:2).

The term "common" is the same word used earlier in the book of Acts in describing the believers who had "all things common" (Acts 4:32). It comes from the Greek word *koinonia*, which means "fellowship" or "in the circle." The gentiles were considered *outside* the circle.

While Peter pondered the meaning of God cleansing the unclean or common animals, three men from Cornelius knocked on the gate where he was staying. The Holy Spirit told Peter to accompany the three to their gentile master's house. Peter had enough sense to obey the Lord.

Once at Cornelius' house, Peter explained the meaning behind the vision he received from God:

> *And he said unto them, Ye know how that it is an unlawful thing for a man that is a Jew to keep company, or come unto one of another nation; but God hath shewed me that I should not call any man common or unclean* (Acts 10:28).

The conclusion of the whole matter was summed up by Peter with these words:

> *... Of a truth I perceive that God is no respecter of persons: But in every nation he that feareth him, and worketh righteousness, is accepted with him* (Acts 10:34,35).

Peter continued preaching, but his preaching was interrupted:

> *While Peter yet spake these words, the Holy Ghost fell on all them which heard the word. And they of the circumcision which believed were astonished, as many as came with Peter, because that on the Gentiles also was poured out the gift of the Holy Ghost* (Acts 10:44,45).

How shocking for the Jews! Two thousand years of separation from among the other nations suddenly fell away. The gentiles were now being grafted into God's good olive tree:

> *For if thou wert cut out of the olive tree which is wild by nature, and wert graffed contrary to nature into a good olive tree: how much more shall these, which be the natural branches, be graffed into their own olive tree? For I would not, brethren, that ye should be ignorant of this mystery, lest ye should be wise in your own conceits; that blindness in part is happened to Israel, until the fulness of the Gentiles be come in* (Romans 11:24,25).

Peter was thoroughly convinced of the Spirit's work in the hearts of Cornelius and his household:

> *Can any man forbid water, that these should not be baptized, which have received the Holy Ghost as well as we?* (Acts 10:47).

The apostle who had been given the "keys of the kingdom" (Matthew 16:19) used them to unlock the door of salvation for the gentiles—but not, as we shall see, without opposition from the Jewish Christians who had comprised the Church up until this time!

OLD HABITS DIE HARD

If you ever thought that Peter was the *undisputed* leader of the New Testament Church, verses 2 and 3 of chapter 11 should dispel that notion:

> *And when Peter was come up to Jerusalem, they that were of the circumcision contended with him, Saying, Thou wentest in to men uncircumcised, and didst eat with them* (Acts 11:2,3).

For ten or eleven years the Christian Church was purely Jewish. It had obviously never occurred to any of the disciples to preach the gospel to the gentiles—despite abundant scriptures which indicated that such was God's plan. Generation after generation of Jews had prided themselves on living a separated life—partitioned from the *common* gentiles. The Cross, however, had broken down all that had previously divided Jew and gentile:

> *For he* [Jesus] *is our peace, who hath made both* [Jew and gentile] *one, and hath broken down the middle wall of partition between us; Having abolished in his flesh the enmity, even the law of commandments contained in ordinances; for to make in himself of twain one new man, so making peace* (Ephesians 2:14,15).

Surrounding the Temple in Jerusalem was a barrier known as "The Middle Wall of Partition." Warnings written in Latin and Greek forbid gentiles from passing any further, upon penalty of death! In Christ there is nothing to divide Jew and gentile any longer; all are made one:

> *There is neither Jew nor Greek, there is neither bond nor free, there is neither male nor female: for ye are all one in Christ Jesus* (Galatians 3:28).

> *Where there is neither Greek nor Jew, circumcision nor uncircumcision, Barbarian, Scythian, bond nor free: but Christ is all, and in all* (Colossians 3:11).

Peter, speaking to the leadership in Jerusalem, had the best defense possible:

> *Forasmuch then as God gave them the like gift as he did unto us, who believed on the Lord Jesus Christ; what was I, that I could withstand God?* (Acts 11:17).

"Look brothers," Peter confidently concluded, "this thing was all of God from start to finish. The Lord gave me the vision of cleansing the unclean animals; the Holy Spirit told me to go to Cornelius' house; the Holy Spirit fell on them before I even finished speaking! What else could I do but go along with what God was doing?"

The disciples recognized that Peter did not act on his own, and the way was opened for an historic shift in the direction of the Church:

When they heard these things, they held their peace, and glorified God, saying, Then hath God also to the Gentiles granted repentance unto life (Acts 11:18).

ANTIOCH: THE NEW CHURCH CENTER

The persecution, which began with the stoning of Stephen, scattered believers throughout the region:

Now they which were scattered abroad upon the persecution that arose about Stephen travelled as far as Phenice [Phoenicia], and Cyprus, and Antioch, preaching the word to none but unto the Jews only (Acts 11:19).

These new Christians preached "the Lord Jesus" (Acts 11:20) to the Jews in the cities where they settled. (See map page 218.) Luke tells us the results of their preaching in Antioch, the city which was destined to become the new center for Christian evangelism through the apostle Paul:

And the hand of the Lord was with them: and a great number believed, and turned unto the Lord (Acts 11:21).

The leadership of the Church in Jerusalem eventually heard about the move of the Spirit in Antioch, and they chose Barnabas to go and investigate. What he saw when he got to Antioch must have impressed him! We're told that he was glad, and this "son of consolation" exhorted the church there to "cleave unto the Lord" (Acts 11:23).

A strong church will always attract unbelievers into its fold; they are drawn by the light, the joy, and the truth. Antioch was no exception:

> . . . *and much people was added unto the Lord* (Acts 11:24).

Barnabas was an exhorter, but not much of a teacher. When each part of the body performs its own function, things run smoothly. Barnabas evidently knew that the new believers in Antioch needed to be grounded in the Word so he set off for Tarsus (see map page 218) to bring back Paul, the master teacher of the Church:

> *And when he had found him, he brought him unto Antioch. And it came to pass, that a whole year they assembled themselves with the church, and taught much people. And the disciples were called Christians first in Antioch* (Acts 11:26).

"Christian" was like a nickname placed on the believers by the *un*believers. "They're always preaching Jesus Christ, Jesus Christ, Jesus Christ; they act like they actually *know* this Jesus Christ!" And so, because of their preaching and witnessing, the Jews and Greeks in the city tagged them with the name "Little Christs."

Things were so "hot" in Antioch that the leaders in Jerusalem decided to send down some of their prophets. Agabus, one of the prophets, foretold of a great famine that would hit Jerusalem and the area of Judea. He passed the test of a true prophet of God:

> *And if thou say in thine heart, How shall we know the word which the LORD hath not spoken? When a prophet speaketh in the name of the LORD, if the thing follow not, nor come to pass, that is the thing which the LORD hath not spoken, but the prophet hath spoken it presumptuously: thou shalt not be afraid of him* (Deuteronomy 18:21,22).

> *The prophet which prophesieth of peace, when the word of the prophet shall come to pass, then shall the prophet be known, that the LORD hath truly sent him* (Jeremiah 28:9).

Just as Agabus had prophesied, a famine did occur. The saints in Antioch took up a collection to help those in Jerusalem. Now it was the new church's turn to help the parent church. The gift was sent with Barnabas and Paul.

DEATH AND DELIVERANCE

At this time in Church history, Herod Agrippa I, the grandson of Herod the Great, was the Roman ruler over

Judea. Herod admired the Jews, and he wanted to please them. And what better way than to persecute the followers of Jesus! Luke tells us that he killed James, the brother of John, which delighted the Jews. Herod thought, "Well, if the death of James made the Jews happy, Peter's death will make them ecstatic!"

Peter was arrested during the time of Passover. The word "Easter" in Acts 12:4 is a mistranslation. It is the Greek word *pascha*, which is translated *Passover* in 26 other places in the New Testament. Herod had Peter guarded around the clock by 16 Roman soldiers, 4 for each of the 4 watches throughout the day and night. During each watch, two of the soldiers were chained to Peter while the other two stood guard. Escape was impossible—or so they thought!

Herod didn't reckon with the Church getting smart fast; this time they prayed:

> *Peter therefore was kept in prison: but prayer was made without ceasing of the church unto God for him* (Acts 12:5).

The prayer was "without ceasing," which is from the Greek word *ektenes* meaning "intense" or "fervent." Peter is the only other person ever to use this word in the New Testament:

> *And above all things have fervent charity among yourselves: for charity shall cover the multitude of sins* (I Peter 4:8).

The believers prayed day and night for Peter; and when the church prayed, God answered:

> *And, behold, the angel of the Lord came upon him* [Peter], *and a light shined in the prison: and he smote Peter on the side, and raised him up, saying, Arise up quickly. And his chains fell off from his hands* (Acts 12:7).

God has guardian angels which work on His behalf for you and me:

> *But to which of the angels said he at any time, Sit on my right hand, until I make thine enemies thy footstool? Are they not all ministering spirits, sent forth to minister for them who shall be heirs of salvation?* (Hebrews 1:13,14).

Peter's guardian angel didn't hang around long; he got the job done and departed. After Peter related the details of his release to the disciples who were gathered at the house of Mary, the mother of John Mark, he also is said to have "departed" (Acts 12:17). This is the last we hear about Peter in the book of Acts with the one exception in Acts 15 at the Jerusalem council. From here on out, the champion of Christianity would be the apostle Paul.

Before Luke took up the account of Paul's calling and travels throughout the Roman Empire, he gave us a contrast between the *words of Herod*, which brought death, and the *Word of God*, which brought life:

And upon a set day Herod, arrayed in royal apparel, sat upon his throne, and made an oration unto them. And immediately the angel of the Lord smote him, because he gave not God the glory: and he was eaten of worms, and gave up the ghost. But the Word of God grew and multiplied (Acts 12:21,23,24).

From this point on we shall see the Word of God spreading from Antioch into town after town, finally reaching its way to Rome. God is very economical: out of the death of James came fervent prayer for Peter, the death of Herod the persecutor, the continued growth of the Christian Church, and the establishment of a base of operation for a missionary movement unlike anything the world had ever seen! It was St. Jerome who said, "The Church of Christ has been founded by shedding its own blood, not that of others; by enduring outrage, not by inflicting it. Persecutions have made it grow; martyrdoms have crowned it." The early Church father Tertullian said simply, "The blood of the martyrs is the seed of the Church." Acts 13-28 gives brilliant testimony to the truth of these words.

CHAPTER SIX

Sticks and Stones
—Building the Church
Through Tribulation
(Acts 13,14)

We have a number of *firsts* in chapter 13: the first missionary journey of Paul (chapters 13 and 14), the first mention of Saul's name change (v. 9), the first recorded sermon by Paul (verses 16-41), and the first formal turn to the gentiles with the gospel by Paul and Barnabas (verse 46). Refer to the map on page 219 as we follow Paul and Barnabas from city to city on their gospel mission. Along the way we'll encounter a sorcerer who is struck blind, the gathering of an entire city to hear Paul speak, signs and wonders, and even a resurrection!

In the last verse of chapter 12, we are told that Barnabas and Paul returned to Antioch from their famine-relief trip to Jerusalem. John Mark came back with them, and there was no doubt a period of one or two years that Paul and Barnabas ministered to the believers in Antioch. When they had proved their faithfulness and as they and the others in the church " . . . *ministered to the Lord, and fasted, . . .* "(Acts 13:2), the Holy Spirit called out Barnabas and Paul to begin a missionary movement that is still going on today.

Let's take a brief look at the other men whom the Holy Spirit mentions in verse 1 of this chapter:

Simeon called Niger: This may have been the man who carried the cross for Jesus:

> *And they compel one Simon a Cyrenian, who passed by, coming out of the country, the father of Alexander and Rufus, to bear his cross* (Mark 15:21).

Paul mentioned Rufus in his letter to the Romans:

> *Salute Rufus chosen in the Lord, and his mother and mine* (Romans 16:13).

Lucius of Cyrene: This may be the Lucius mentioned by Paul:

> *Timotheus my workfellow, and Lucius, and Jason, and Sosipater, my kinsmen, salute you* (Romans 16:21).

Manaen who had been brought up with Herod: This Herod would have been Antipas, whom Jesus called "that fox" (Luke 13:32). This was the Herod who had John the

Baptist beheaded. How sad that while Manaen became a believer, Herod became a beast!

These godly men were evidently the leadership in the church at Antioch. They laid their hands on Barnabas and Paul and sent them out. What a loss those two men must have been to the church there! The church, however, was willing to obey the Holy Spirit and sacrifice for the greater good of God's overall plan of evangelism.

FIRST STOP: CYPRUS

On Paul's second and third missionary journeys, he headed north from Antioch into Cilicia and Galatia; but on this first journey with Barnabas, they headed south to the seaport of Seleucia and then set sail to Cyprus. Why? Barnabas was from Cyprus; and don't you know that he would be eager to share the good news with family, friends, and acquaintances there!

Verse 5 of this chapter shows us the initial pattern that Barnabas and Paul followed whenever they went into a city:

And when they were at Salamis, they preached the word of God in the synagogues of the Jews: and they had also John to their minister (Acts 13:5).

Salamis must have been a bustling city, with more than one synagogue. There was always a time during the Saturday gathering when visitors were acknowledged and given the opportunity to share a greeting and news from other cities.

What a perfect setup! Luke tells us that Barnabas and Paul preached "the word of God" to the Jews. We're also told that John Mark came along to minister to Barnabas and Paul. *Minister* is the Greek word *huperetes* which is a nautical term meaning "a rower on a ship." John Mark came along to provide for the personal needs of the apostles.

Barnabas, Paul, and John Mark walked the length of the island, no doubt preaching as they went; and they finally ended up at the city of Paphos on the southwestern end of the isle. A temple to Venus, the goddess of love, stood in or near Paphos; and she was worshiped as the "Queen of Paphos." Every woman in Cyprus, once during her lifetime, was required to offer herself in prostitution at the temple. The money from this abominable practice went to further the worship of Venus and to the priests who were the custodians of the temple. This was the heathen society that the gospel was taken into by Barnabas and Paul!

The island of Cyprus was governed by Rome from the city of Paphos. The proconsul in charge was one Sergius Paulus. Obviously this man had some kind of interest in the things of God or he wouldn't have sent for Barnabas and Paul and desired to hear the Word of God from their lips.

Opposition to the gospel message came from a backslidden Jew named Bar-jesus who evidently had some kind of association with the proconsul. Bar-jesus also went by the name *Elymas*, which means "enlightened one." Far from being enlightened, this Jew had turned his back on the light of God found in His Word. Bar-jesus actively sought to turn

Sergius Paulus away from the truth taught by Barnabas and Paul, but he had never met anyone like Paul:

> *Then Saul, (who also is called Paul,) filled with the Holy Ghost, set his eyes on him, And said, O full of all subtilty and all mischief, thou child of the devil, thou enemy of all righteousness, wilt thou not cease to pervert the right ways of the Lord?* (Acts 13:9,10).

Paul was not about to be intimidated by anyone of any rank, position, or persuasion. Speaking by the inspiration of the Holy Spirit, Paul pronounced blindness for a season upon the "enlightened" one. This miracle confirmed the gospel message preached by Paul and Barnabas and resulted in the salvation of Sergius Paulus—the "prudent" Roman governor of Cyprus!

THE CHURCH IN TURKEY

Verse 13 of chapter 13 mentions " . . . Paul and his company . . . " leaving Cyprus and crossing over to what is modern-day Turkey. From this point on it is Paul who is usually mentioned ahead of Barnabas in the narrative. They landed at Perga, which was the capital city of the region of Pamphylia. It was here that John Mark departed from Paul and Barnabas and returned to his home in Jerusalem.

We are simply not told the reasons for John Mark's defection. Was he homesick? Did Paul lay out his plans for walking miles and miles through the mountainous terrain and thief-riddled roads leading to Antioch, Iconium, Lystra, and Derbe? Did John Mark's commitment waver? Whatever the reason, his departure would later create serious contention between Paul and Barnabas and eventually lead to their separation.

The seriousness of John Mark's defection can be seen in Luke's use of the word "departing" in verse 13; this word is used only two other times in the New Testament—both in a negative light:

> *And then will I profess unto them, I never knew you: depart from me, ye that work iniquity* (Matthew 7:23).

> *And, lo, a spirit taketh him, and he suddenly crieth out; and it teareth him that he foameth again, and bruising him hardly departeth from him* (Luke 9:39).

Leaving Perga, Paul and Barnabas traveled to Pisidia Antioch, another capital city. As was their custom, Paul and Barnabas went to the synagogue and waited for their opportunity to speak. Sure enough, the rulers of the synagogue asked them if they had any word of exhortation (Acts 13:15); and Paul wasted no time with pleasantries but dove into a lengthy recap of Jewish history right down to John the Baptist and Jesus Himself.

"The crucifixion of Jesus fulfilled the words of the prophets," Paul concluded. "Jesus' resurrection was verified by many eyewitnesses and was another fulfillment of prophecy." Paul's message ended with some hard words about the Law of Moses and a warning against rejecting the forgiveness being offered:

> *Be it known unto you therefore, men and brethren, that through this man is preached unto you the forgiveness of sins: And by him all that believe are justified from all things, from which ye could not be justified by the law of Moses. Beware therefore, lest that come upon you, which is spoken of in the prophets; Behold, ye despisers, and wonder, and perish: for I work a work in your days, a work which ye shall in no wise believe, though a man declare it unto you* (Acts 13:38-41).

As always, there were two reactions to Paul's preaching; in this instance most of those who were of pure Jewish blood left the synagogue in a huff while some Jews and the gentile proselytes to Judaism wanted to hear more about Jesus. The news about Paul and his gospel spread throughout the town, and the following Saturday "almost the whole city" gathered to hear Paul preach (Acts 13:44).

When the Jews saw the multitude that followed after Paul and Barnabas, the Scripture says that envy moved them to argue against the truth and actually blaspheme God. This wasn't the first time that envy had motivated religious men to action:

*Therefore when they were gathered together,
Pilate said unto them, Whom will ye that I release
unto you? Barabbas, or Jesus which is called
Christ? For he knew that for envy they had
delivered him* (Matthew 27:17,18).

*Then the high priest rose up, and all they that
were with him, (which is the sect of the Sadducees,)
and were filled with indignation* [envy]
(Acts 5:17).

THE TURN TO
THE GENTILES

This stiffnecked rejection by the Jews produced a
dramatic turning point in the apostles' ministry:

*Then Paul and Barnabas waxed bold, and said,
It was necessary that the word of God should first
have been spoken to you: but seeing ye put it
from you, and judge yourselves unworthy of
everlasting life, lo, we turn to the Gentiles*
(Acts 13:46).

A quote from the prophet Isaiah flashed through Paul's
mind and gave him fresh direction and inspiration for his
God-given mission:

*For so hath the Lord commanded us, saying, I
have set thee to be a light of the Gentiles, that thou*

shouldest be for salvation unto the ends of the earth (Acts 13:47).

And he said, It is a light thing that thou shouldest be my servant to raise up the tribes of Jacob, and to restore the preserved of Israel: I will also give thee for a light to the Gentiles, that thou mayest be my salvation unto the end of the earth (Isaiah 49:6).

Naturally this made the gentiles happy:

And when the Gentiles heard this, they were glad, and glorified the word of the Lord: and as many as were ordained to eternal life believed. And the word of the Lord was published throughout all the region (Acts 13:48,49).

Notice that it was the Word of the Lord that was glorified and published and not the word of Paul or Barnabas. There were those, however, who felt that Paul's message was his own. They stirred up some of the leading men and women in the city and "expelled" God's messengers. Paul and Barnabas shook the dust off their feet as a testimony against the unbelievers:

And whosoever shall not receive you, nor hear you, when ye depart thence, shake off the dust under your feet for a testimony against them. Verily I say unto you, It shall be more tolerable for Sodom and Gomorrha in the day of judgment, than for that city (Mark 6:11).

Their expulsion was nothing less than what Jesus had warned His disciples to expect:

> *Behold, I send you forth as sheep in the midst of wolves: be ye therefore wise as serpents, and harmless as doves. But beware of men: for they will deliver you up to the councils, and they will scourge you in their synagogues* (Matthew 10:16,17).

Hardships and adverse circumstances, however, could not affect the inward peace and happiness that Paul and Barnabas had found in their relationship to the living God:

> *And the disciples were filled with joy, and with the Holy Ghost* (Acts 13:52).

ON TO ICONIUM

Despite their "turn to the Gentiles" proclaimed at Antioch, Paul and Barnabas once again used the forum of the Jewish synagogue to spread their message at Iconium, the capital of a region known as Lycaonia. Their ministry was so powerful and persuasive in the Holy Spirit that " . . . *a great multitude both of the Jews and also of the Greeks believed"* (Acts 14:1). The unbelieving Jews, however, once again stirred up opposition; but this time the Lord performed signs and wonders through the hands of Paul and Barnabas to confirm His message and His messengers. Luke records that Paul and Barnabas stayed at Iconium a "long time" to encourage and build up the believers in the faith.

Eventually the city was sharply divided into two camps: believers and unbelievers. The apostles were made aware of a plot to stone them. They could have stayed and relied on the Lord's protection, but they chose to take their message to Lystra, a city composed largely of gentile idolaters. No mention is made of Paul and Barnabas preaching in the Jewish synagogues in Lystra or Derbe, and their ministry met with much acceptance at both towns.

It was at Lystra that we have the first recorded miracle of healing by Paul:

> *And there sat a certain man at Lystra, impotent in his feet, being a cripple from his mother's womb, who never had walked: The same heard Paul speak: who stedfastly beholding him, and perceiving that he had faith to be healed, Said with a loud voice, Stand upright on thy feet. And he leaped and walked* (Acts 14:8-10).

As a result of this miracle, Paul and Barnabas faced an entirely different problem than they had experienced in Antioch or Iconium: the pagan crowd tried to worship and offer sacrifices to them! The citizens of Lystra worshiped the planets and had their own temple to Jupiter. Paul refused their worship and took the opportunity to speak against the vain practice of worshiping the creation instead of the Creator:

> *And saying, Sirs, why do ye these things? We also are men of like passions with you, and preach unto you that ye should turn from these vanities*

113

unto the living God, which made heaven, and
earth, and the sea, and all things that are therein
(Acts 14:15).

No doubt the people would have been willing to hear more
from Paul and Barnabas, but Jews from Antioch and
Iconium were so enraged at Paul that they followed him to
Lystra and turned the people against him:

And there came thither certain Jews from Antioch
and Iconium, who persuaded the people, and,
having stoned Paul, drew him out of the city,
supposing he had been dead (Acts 14:19).

Bible scholars have a difference of opinion as to whether
Paul was actually dead at this time or merely unconscious.
I personally believe he was dead. A group of disciples stood
around Paul, no doubt praying for him; and Luke tells us
that "he rose up" and was taken back into the city. The
Greek word for "rose up" is *anistemi*, and it is used
111 times in the New Testament with around 35 of those
instances referring to bodily resurrection.

Paul's resurrection was absolutely supernatural. How do
I know? Because verse 20 says that the very next day he
headed out with Barnabas to Derbe, some 18 miles away
by foot! Paul did not despise the persecution he suffered,
but rather identified more closely with the suffering of
his Savior:

From henceforth let no man trouble me: for I

bear in my body the marks of the Lord Jesus (Galatians 6:17).

Was Paul intimidated by his persecutors? Was he reluctant to speak out for fear of offending his listeners? No way! As soon as he and Barnabas arrived in Derbe they *". . . preached the gospel to that city, . . ."* (Acts 14:21). And after they finished making disciples in Derbe, they headed right back to Lystra! Paul cared more about the saints than the stones, retracing his steps so that he could strengthen the new believers in their faith amidst a hostile culture:

Confirming the souls of the disciples, and exhorting them to continue in the faith, and that we must through much tribulation enter the kingdom of God. And when they had ordained them elders in every church, and had prayed with fasting, they commended them to the Lord, on whom they believed (Acts 14:22,23).

ORGANIZING THE CHURCHES

Elders were ordained in the churches that Paul and Barnabas established. The qualifications for this office are given by Paul in his letters to Timothy and Titus:

This is a true saying, If a man desire the office of a bishop, he desireth a good work. A bishop then must be blameless, the husband of one wife, vigilant, sober, of good behaviour, given to hospitality, apt to teach; Not given to wine, no striker, not greedy of filthy lucre; but patient, not a brawler, not covetous; One that ruleth well his own house, having his children in subjection with all gravity; (For if a man know not how to rule his own house, how shall he take care of the church of God?) Not a novice, lest being lifted up with pride he fall into the condemnation of the devil. Moreover he must have a good report of them which are without; lest he fall into reproach and the snare of the devil (I Timothy 3:1-7).

For this cause left I [Paul] *thee in Crete, that thou shouldest set in order the things that are wanting, and ordain elders in every city, as I had appointed thee: If any be blameless, the husband of one wife, having faithful children not accused of riot or unruly. For a bishop must be blameless, as the steward of God; not selfwilled, not soon angry, not given to wine, no striker, not given to filthy lucre; But a lover of hospitality, a lover of good men, sober, just, holy, temperate; Holding fast the faithful word as he hath been taught, that he may be able by sound doctrine both to exhort and to convince the gainsayers* (Titus 1:5-9).

Paul left the churches in good hands, but beyond that, he " . . . *commended them to the Lord,* . . . " (Acts 14:23). After all is said and done on the human level, we must trust to the grace and goodness of God to carry on His work in the hearts of men. Paul's trust was in the power of God and His Word to sustain and nourish the new believers.

The path back to Syrian Antioch and their home church included another time of preaching in Perga and then the 12-mile walk to catch a ship at Attalia. Once at home they recited " . . . *all that God had done . . .* " in opening the door of faith to the gentiles (Acts 14:27). Thus, established churches had been set up in several key cities; and Paul's message of God's salvation through faith apart from Jewish law or tradition had been tested in the hottest furnaces. But a different gospel was being preached in Jerusalem by some; and Paul, together with Barnabas, would face yet another test of doctrine—this time with the leadership of the church in Jerusalem.

CHAPTER SEVEN

Decision Time —the Church Confronts the Legalists
(Acts 15:1-35)

A cts 15 is one of the most important chapters in the book of Acts. The issue decided at what is commonly known as the "Jerusalem Council" has been a foundation throughout the Church age. The contention was so strong that it easily could have divided the New Testament Church into two factions of Jewish and gentile believers. Verse one tells us the crux of the matter:

> *And certain men which came down from Judea taught the brethren, and said, Except ye be circumcised after the manner of Moses, ye cannot be saved* (Acts 15:1).

Paul made reference to these men in his letter to the Galatians:

For before that certain came from James he [Peter]
did eat with the Gentiles: but when they were
come, he withdrew and separated himself, fearing
them which were from the circumcision
(Galatians 2:12).

Imagine the influence these visitors had: they were from
Jerusalem, the "mother" church; they came in the name
of James, one of the leading apostles of the church and the
half-brother of Jesus. These Jewish believers were teaching
that if the gentiles were not circumcised, they were
not saved.

The church at Antioch was a very free church, having
Jews *and* gentiles who had been born again. They moved
together, they flowed together, they had the same vision
for the kingdom. But when the visitors arrived from the
church in Jerusalem, the Jewish believers at Antioch
refused to eat with their gentile brothers and sisters. The
Jewish believers held on to the ritual requirements of the
Mosaic law, and it became a very serious situation in the
church at Antioch with repercussions for the Church
worldwide.

FAITH PLUS WORKS?

The principle under attack here was salvation by faith
alone. It was a conflict between faith *plus* circumcision or
faith without circumcision. It was a conflict between the
ritual law and the spiritual law. It was a conflict between
flesh and spirit. It brought much dissension because it

attempted to mix grace with law. Paul saw the seriousness of it in overturning the purity of God's purpose in sending Jesus to the cross. There was strong dissension, and it looked like there could be an insurrection in the Church.

Strife was ripping up the Antioch church, and isn't this Satan's way? If the devil can get Christians fighting among themselves, they will have no energy to reach the world for Christ. It is the enemy's favorite tactic, and it is still used today in the Christian Church.

The Antioch church finally decided that the matter would have to be solved in Jerusalem by the apostles and elders. The problem had originated in Jerusalem, and so it would be dealt with there.

Paul and Barnabas went to Jerusalem and declared the wonderful things that God had been doing among the gentiles, or the uncircumcised:

> *Then all the multitude kept silence, and gave audience to Barnabas and Paul, declaring what miracles and wonders God had wrought among the Gentiles by them* (Acts 15:12).

The gentiles had been saved without the rite of circumcision. These Jewish teachers who were teaching that the gentiles had to be circumcised in order to be saved were born-again Pharisees. They believed in Jesus as Messiah, but they believed that gentiles must be circumcised and they must keep the law. They were very legalistic. They had missed the spirit of the law:

For circumcision verily profiteth, if thou keep the law: but if thou be a breaker of the law, thy circumcision is made uncircumcision. Therefore if the uncircumcision keep the righteousness of the law, shall not his uncircumcision be counted for circumcision? And shall not uncircumcision which is by nature, if it fulfil the law, judge thee, who by the letter and circumcision dost transgress the law? For he is not a Jew, which is one outwardly; neither is that circumcision, which is outward in the flesh: But he is a Jew, which is one inwardly; and circumcision is that of the heart, in the spirit, and not in the letter; whose praise is not of men, but of God (Romans 2:25-29).*

If you look at the attack that Satan was trying to make on the Church, you can see that the Church could have died right at this point. If they had made the decision that all gentiles had to be circumcised and had to keep the Mosaic law, that would have been the end of the Church. The Church would simply have been a small group of Jewish believers.

Time was very short. If this conference at Jerusalem took place around 50 A.D., within the next eight years Paul would be arrested. Shortly after that would be the great fire of Rome, and Nero would use Christians as scapegoats—they would be persecuted ruthlessly. In 70 A.D. the destruction of Jerusalem would be completed. If the gentile world was not evangelized quickly, there would have been no strong foundation from which to grow outside Jerusalem.

When Paul and Barnabas arrived in Jerusalem, I am sure they were looked upon with skepticism, even though Paul had been there before (this was his third visit to Jerusalem). Certainly Paul understood the Pharisees; he had been one. The Pharisees believed in resurrection, so it probably was not too difficult for them to believe in the resurrection of Jesus. The Sadducees did not believe in a resurrection of any kind. So it was harder for Sadducees to become believers. But the converted Pharisees seemed to remain legalistic at heart. They were becoming a Jewish sect in the Christian Church.

First of all, the Pharisees presented the case for circumcision. Here are some points in favor of circumcision:

1. Circumcision was given before the law to Abraham. It was God's seal of His covenant with Abraham (Genesis 17; Romans 4:11). Those who did not receive circumcision were cut off. They were not covenant believers; they didn't have covenant promises. Circumcision was actually called the "covenant of circumcision":

> *And he gave him the covenant of circumcision: and so Abraham begat Isaac, and circumcised him the eighth day; and Isaac begat Jacob; and Jacob begat the twelve patriarchs* (Acts 7:8).

2. Circumcision was very serious to the Lord—Moses was almost killed because one of his children had not been circumcised:

And it came to pass by the way in the inn, that the LORD met him, and sought to kill him. Then Zipporah took a sharp stone, and cut off the foreskin of her son, and cast it at his feet, and said, Surely a bloody husband art thou to me. So he let him go: then she said, A bloody husband thou art, because of the circumcision (Exodus 4:24-26).

3. Moses confirmed circumcision (Exodus 12:43-50; Joshua 5:1-10). No one was allowed to partake in the Passover without circumcision. To Jews, there were just two classes of people in the whole world: the circumcised and the uncircumcised. The Jews always believed that if you were going to have covenant blessings, you had to be circumcised. That was the sign of the covenant.

PETER TO THE DEFENSE

Peter, who was sent to the circumcision (the Jews), gave one of the best arguments *against* circumcision. Peter shared the full testimony of his preaching and teaching in the home of Cornelius (Acts 10). Peter told how the Holy Spirit was given to the gentiles just as it was to the Jews. God had made no difference; their hearts were purified by faith. In Acts 15:10 Peter said that the law was a yoke of bondage. Jesus had said: *"Take my yoke upon you, . . . For my yoke is easy, and my burden is light"* (Matthew 11:29,30).

Paul taught the Galatians about the yoke of bondage:

Stand fast therefore in the liberty wherewith Christ hath made us free, and be not entangled again with the yoke of bondage (Galatians 5:1).

When we come to Jesus, we find out that the law of circumcision was a yoke of bondage to the flesh. But when we take His yoke, we have the yoke of His grace. The Jews were saved by faith, and the gentiles were saved by faith. It was a work of the Holy Spirit.

Jesus had described the heavy burdens of the Pharisees:

For they bind heavy burdens and grievous to be borne, and lay them on men's shoulders; but they themselves will not move them with one of their fingers (Matthew 23:4).

The rabbis continued to add little pieces of law to the commandments until they were such a load that no man could carry them. Paul even told about how he could not keep the 10th commandment concerning evil desires (Romans 7:15-23). Only Jesus kept the law. If all of these "burdens" had been put upon the gentiles, it would have driven them to destruction. Peter's question was, "Why should the Church fasten on the new gentile believers' shoulders the yoke of the law? Jesus came to set them free. The Jews have never been able to do it; how could they expect the gentiles to keep it?" The law puts the load on man, but grace puts the load on Christ. The two can never be compatible.

After Peter testified (verse 12), Barnabas and Paul began. Of course, they had seen firsthand what was happening among the gentiles. They knew that God was at work mightily. Paul, who was the greatest legalist of all, received the greatest revelation of grace. We can still read his words concerning grace in Romans 4 and in the book of Galatians.

Paul no doubt spoke of Abraham, the father of all who believed. Before Abraham was circumcised, God had given him the promise. Before Abraham received circumcision and *after* Abraham received circumcision, he walked in faith. And this was not the Abrahamic Covenant, this was the New Covenant:

> *That the blessing of Abraham might come on the Gentiles through Jesus Christ; that we might receive the promise of the Spirit through faith* (Galatians 3:14).

Paul later had Timothy circumcised (Acts 16:3), and yet he did not allow Titus to be circumcised (Galatians 2:3). He gave his reasons for this:

> *And unto the Jews I became as a Jew, that I might gain the Jews; to them that are under the law, as under the law, that I might gain them that are under the law; To them that are without law, as without law, (being not without law to God, but under the law to Christ,) that I might gain them that are without law* (I Corinthians 9:20,21).

There was no question that Paul and Barnabas had the greatest revelation of what God was doing among the gentiles, since they had seen it firsthand. Peter had a taste, but Paul and Barnabas had a whole meal.

Now James spoke (verses 13-21). James put super importance on God's Word. He quoted from Amos 9:11,12. Peter had quoted from Joel on the day of Pentecost, showing the Jews the prophecy of the outpouring of the Holy Spirit. James quoted from Amos, showing the Jews that the outpouring of the Holy Spirit on the gentiles had placed them into the New Covenant. Amos had prophesied that God would again build the Tabernacle of David so that the gentiles would come into it:

JAMES	AMOS
And to this agree the words of the prophets; as it is written, After this I will return, and will build again the tabernacle of David, which is fallen down; and I will build again the ruins thereof, and I will set it up: That the residue of men might seek after the Lord, and all the Gentiles, upon whom my name is called, saith the Lord, who doeth all these things (Acts 15:15-17).	*In that day will I raise up the tabernacle of David that is fallen, and close up the breaches thereof; and I will raise up his ruins, and I will build it as in the days of old: That they may possess the remnant of Edom, and of all the heathen, which are called by my name, saith the* LORD *that doeth this* (Amos 9:11,12).

THE TABERNACLE OF MOSES OR DAVID?

The Jews had been under the Mosaic Covenant, and they knew the Tabernacle of Moses. But the gentiles would not come into the Tabernacle of *Moses* (which represented the law), they would come into the Tabernacle of *David*. They were coming into the newer covenant by faith in the son of David, Jesus Christ. They came into a new priesthood after the order of Melchizedek. They would be a part of a spiritual house.

The Tabernacle of David has a most interesting history. In I Chronicles 15,16,17, we see that David established a new order of worship in the Tabernacle. He placed the Tabernacle at Mount Zion. The Tabernacle of Moses had been at Mount Gibeon, but David moved it (I Chronicles 16:37-43; II Chronicles 1:3,13). So the Tabernacle of Moses still had priests who ministered there, but now David had other priests who were ministering at his Tabernacle. David had taken the Ark of the Covenant out of the Tabernacle of Moses and placed it in his Tabernacle—the Tabernacle of David. We know that the Ark of the Covenant typified God's glory; thus the glory had been removed from the Mosaic Tabernacle and put into David's Tabernacle.

There was a new order of worship in David's Tabernacle. There was singing and praising and joy and thanksgiving. The Tabernacle of Moses simply had its outer-court functions. The priest couldn't go into the Holy of Holies—

128

there was no Ark of the Covenant. The great sacrifices of David's Tabernacle were the sacrifices of praise.

All this has a parallel in the New Testament. When Jesus died, the veil of the Temple was torn in two:

> *And, behold, the veil of the temple was rent in twain from the top to the bottom; and the earth did quake, and the rocks rent* (Matthew 27:51).

This showed that God's presence had changed to His new place of habitation—to the Church, the Temple of the living God, built up with living stones. The Tabernacle of Moses and the law of covenants stemmed from Mount Sinai. But we have not come to Mount Sinai; we have come to Mount Zion:

> *For ye are not come unto the mount that might be touched, and that burned with fire, nor unto blackness, and darkness, and tempest, . . . But ye are come unto mount Sion, and unto the city of the living God, the heavenly Jerusalem, and to an innumerable company of angels* (Hebrews 12:18,22).

I absolutely love the way James was able to quote from the little book of Amos to verify what Paul and Barnabas shared concerning the salvation of the gentiles. Acts 10 (the salvation of Cornelius' household) was the fulfilment of Amos' prophecy regarding the reestablishment of David's Tabernacle and the coming in of the gentiles into God's house by faith apart from the law. James knew that he could not go against the Scriptures; his conclusion is found beginning in Acts 15:19:

> *Wherefore my sentence is, that we trouble not them, which from among the Gentiles are turned to God: But that we write unto them, that they abstain from pollutions of idols, and from fornication, and from things strangled, and from blood* (Acts 15:19,20).

The gentiles were indeed turning to God, but earlier James had pointed out that it was God Who was choosing the gentiles to become a part of the Church:

> *Simeon hath declared how God at the first did visit the Gentiles, to take out of them a people for his name* (Acts 15:14).

That's what the Church is all about—God calling out a people for His name. The word *ekklesia* means a "called out assembly." God has a calling-out process. It began at Pentecost with the Jews. Then He called out Cornelius' household, and He continued with other gentiles. Paul and Barnabas had gone to the land of the gentiles calling out people for God's Church. God is still calling out Jews and gentiles; these are His Church.

The decree of James was that the gentiles had come into the Body of Christ apart from the law and thus were not under the yoke of circumcision. They were not under the Mosaic Covenant; they were in the New Covenant—the way of salvation, which is faith in Christ Jesus.

James gave specific instructions for the gentile believers. These instructions were not severe; they were designed to unite the Jew and the gentile to Christ. James decreed that they must preach Jesus, not Moses. God had said that Jesus was His beloved Son and that men were to listen to Him. Moses and Elijah had pointed to Jesus. The Church must exalt Jesus.

James and the other apostles at Jerusalem wrote letters to send back with Paul, Barnabas, Judas, and Silas. There is a four-fold aspect to these letters:

Spiritual Relationship
1. Abstain from meat offered to idols (I Corinthians 8:1-13).

2. Abstain from blood (Genesis 9:4; Leviticus 17:10-14). This was first mentioned in the Noahic Covenant and later confirmed in the Mosaic Covenant.

Brotherly Relationship
3. Abstain from things strangled (Leviticus 22:8). Undoubtedly this had to do with their Jewish relationships. In following this admonition they would not be a stumbling block to their Jewish brothers.

Physical Relationship
4. Abstain from fornication (I Corinthians 5:13, 6:13-20, 7:2). They were to be morally clean.

The gentiles had lived in much sexual impurity and idolatry. Immorality and uncleanness were forbidden by all nine of God's covenants.

Now the letter had to be taken and read to believers in other churches. One of the men, Judas Barsabas, was perhaps the brother of Joseph Barsabas, who was a candidate to succeed Judas Iscariot (Acts 1:23). *Barsabas* means "son of the Sabbath." The other man was Silas, who was a citizen of Rome (Acts 16:37). He was an elder in this early Jerusalem church. Later we see that he went on the mission field with Paul. Sometimes Silas is called Silvanus.

Now the Church knew the truth: true circumcision was of the heart and not of the flesh. Acts 7:8 speaks of the "covenant of circumcision" that God made with Abraham. In the New Testament the covenant of circumcision is a covenant in the heart and in the spirit, but not in the flesh and of the letter. God looks for the new creature, the one whose heart has been circumcised:

> *Therefore if any man be in Christ, he is a new creature: old things are passed away; behold, all things are become new* (II Corinthians 5:17).

The Holy Spirit performs spiritual circumcision in our hearts:

> *In whom also ye are circumcised with the circumcision made without hands, in putting off the body of the sins of the flesh by the circumcision of Christ: Buried with him in baptism, wherein also ye are risen with him through the faith of the operation of God, who hath raised him from the dead* (Colossians 2:11,12).

From the human standpoint the Church had passed a crucial test. Of course from God's viewpoint the outcome was sure all along because Jesus had said, "... *I will build my church; and the gates of hell shall not prevail against it*" (Matthew 16:18). Notice how Paul was willing to trust the Holy Spirit in this matter. In the natural no one would have thought that the leadership in Jerusalem would abandon its strong legalistic ways. But God is bigger than all the plans of men; we need to trust that His Spirit and His Word will emerge triumphant in every situation.

Now that the Church was one, the gospel would be taken into a new continent—Europe. Paul's second missionary journey is filled with the supernatural: demons cast out, a great earthquake, and the conversion of an entire household in the middle of the night!

CHAPTER EIGHT

The Gospel Goes to Europe —and a Jittery Jailer Meets Jesus
(Acts 15:36-16:40)

Paul could have stayed in Antioch and built a thriving ministry there; but his heart was with the men, women, and children whose faces he remembered from his first missionary journey. Paul loved the churches that he had begun; he spoke of their care in his letter to the Corinthians:

> *Beside those things that are without, that which cometh upon me daily, the care of all the churches* (II Corinthians 11:28).

Paul had founded these churches—they were his children. He and Barnabas began to make preparations to retrace the steps of their first trip abroad with the gospel, but they came into sharp contention because Paul did not want John Mark to accompany them again:

But Paul thought not good to take him [John Mark]
with them, who departed from them from
Pamphylia, and went not with them to the work.
And the contention was so sharp between them,
that they departed asunder one from the other:
and so Barnabas took Mark, and sailed unto
Cyprus (Acts 15:38,39).

Paul would become a great developer of young men and
women, but John Mark would not be one of them—
Barnabas and Peter would develop him. Paul developed
people such as Luke, Gaius, Timothy, Silas, Tychicus, and
Trophimus. However, the last letter penned by Paul would
forever set the record straight concerning the character of
John Mark:

Only Luke is with me. Take Mark, and bring him
with thee: for he is profitable to me for the
ministry (II Timothy 4:11).

God is certainly the God of second chances; and under
the leadership of Barnabas (and later Peter), John Mark was
used by the Lord to minister not only to the apostle Paul
but also to write one of the four gospels!

PAUL CHOOSES SILAS

Paul took Silas with him. Silas was a chief man among
the church in Jerusalem:

Then pleased it the apostles and elders, with the whole church, to send chosen men of their own company to Antioch with Paul and Barnabas; namely, Judas surnamed Barsabas, and Silas, chief men among the brethren (Acts 15:22).

All four (Paul, Silas, Barnabas, and Mark) were sent forth by the church with the grace of God (Acts 15:40). God's grace would work in them all. Paul and Silas went through Syria and Cilicia, confirming the churches. (Refer to the map on page 220 for the locations mentioned in this chapter.) Not much is heard about Barnabas after this time; our attention has been passed to Paul. We are not told whether Paul stopped at his home town of Tarsus, but in all probability he would be eager to stop there and share the gospel with friends and relatives.

The churches established on Paul's first trip were thriving; and, of course, a copy of the Jerusalem letter was left with each church. Paul and Silas were there to confirm what was written in the letter.

TIMOTHY JOINS THE TEAM

When they arrived at Lystra, Paul encountered Timothy—a very promising young man who had been converted when Paul and Barnabas traveled through Lystra on the first missionary trip.

Timothy was the son of a Jewish mother and a Greek father. It appears that Timothy had been raised by his mother Eunice and Lois, his grandmother. Both were godly women; and consequently, Timothy was brought up more a Jew than a gentile. Paul mentions Timothy's background in a letter:

> *When I call to remembrance the unfeigned faith that is in thee, which dwelt first in thy grand-mother Lois, and thy mother Eunice; and I am persuaded that in thee also* (II Timothy 1:5).

Lystra, Timothy's hometown, was the place where Paul was stoned on his first missionary journey. It is interesting that when Stephen was stoned, Paul became the fruit of Stephen's stoning. Paul was stoned at Lystra, and it appears that Timothy became the fruit of Paul's stoning:

> *Unto Timothy, my own son in the faith: Grace, mercy, and peace, from God our Father and Jesus Christ our Lord* (I Timothy 1:2).

> *Paul, an apostle of Jesus Christ by the will of God, according to the promise of life which is in Christ Jesus, To Timothy, my dearly beloved son: Grace, mercy, and peace, from God the Father and Christ Jesus our Lord* (II Timothy 1:1,2).

> *Thou therefore, my son, be strong in the grace that is in Christ Jesus* (II Timothy 2:1).

> *But thou* [Timothy] *hast fully known my doctrine, manner of life, purpose, faith, longsuffering, charity, patience, Persecutions, afflictions, which came unto me at Antioch, at Iconium, at Lystra; what persecutions I endured: but out of them all the Lord delivered me* (II Timothy 3:10,11).

Timothy had proved himself faithful in a local church before Paul took him along to train him and to use him in ministry. Timothy received his ministry through prophecy and the laying on of hands:

> *This charge I commit unto thee, son Timothy, according to the prophecies which went before on thee, that thou by them mightest war a good warfare* (I Timothy 1:18).

> *Neglect not the gift that is in thee, which was given thee by prophecy, with the laying on of the hands of the presbytery* (I Timothy 4:14).

> *Wherefore I put thee in remembrance that thou stir up the gift of God, which is in thee by the putting on of my hands* (II Timothy 1:6).

CIRCUMCISION OR UNCIRCUMCISION?

The Jerusalem Council had decided that circumcision was NOT a requirement for gentiles to be saved. Paul stood firmly on the side of those who came to that conclusion. Why then, many people ask, did Paul have Timothy circumcised? Timothy, in a sense, because he was not circumcised, was neither Jew nor gentile. Because Timothy's mother was a Jewess, Paul felt that it was good to have him circumcised so that Timothy could also minister to the Jews. It wasn't that circumcision was a requirement to preach the gospel, but it did make for more openness on the part of the Jews when Paul and Timothy spoke:

> *For in Christ Jesus neither circumcision availeth any thing, nor uncircumcision, but a new creature* (Galatians 6:15).

> *For though I be free from all men, yet have I made myself servant unto all, that I might gain the more. And unto the Jews I became as a Jew, that I might gain the Jews; to them that are under the law, as under the law, that I might gain them that are under the law* (I Corinthians 9:19,20).

As Paul, Silas, and Timothy began their trip, we read about their search for the leading of the Holy Spirit. They were "forbidden" of the Holy Spirit to go to Asia (Acts 16:6), and the Spirit "suffered them not" to go into the region of Bithynia (Acts 16:7). The Holy Spirit has to prepare men's hearts before the Word can be effectively preached, and it was not the right time. Paul did not try to force the issue. There are timings for cities as well as timings for people.

Paul seemed to be constantly leading his team westward, always listening for the still small voice of God. It must have been a difficult time of wonder for them. We always have to follow the Lord of the harvest because He knows where the harvest is!

When Paul arrived at Troas, (which was a very important city with a big harbor that linked Macedonia, Greece, and Europe), he stopped. This was a very strategic place where Paul needed to hear from the Holy Spirit. Paul received a vision in the night; a man from Macedonia called Paul to come over and to help him. This would prove to be a turning point in church history. Paul would go westward into Europe, and the West would be evangelized first. If Paul had gone eastward, India and China would have been first. God sovereignly chose the path for the gospel.

Notice that Paul obeyed *immediately*:

> *And after he had seen the vision, immediately we endeavoured to go into Macedonia, assuredly gathering that the Lord had called us for to preach the gospel unto them* (Acts 16:10).

LUKE JOINS THE TEAM

The "we" in Acts 16:10 must include Luke, the author of Acts. This is the first mention of "we," and many Bible scholars feel that Luke must have joined Paul's team during the layover in Troas. The group left Troas and stopped overnight at Samothracia, an island that jutted up out of the Aegean Sea to a height of 5,000 feet. It was midway between Troas and Neapolis (the seaport serving the city of Philippi which was some ten miles inland).

Philippi was the chief city in this part of Macedonia. Luke seemed to like Philippi; he stayed there for some years. Philippi was a colonial city, an outpost of the Roman Empire. Rome ruled the world through her colonies.

FIRST CONVERTS IN EUROPE

On the first sabbath day after he arrived, Paul went outside the city to a riverside area used for worship (there may not have been a synagogue in Philippi). God opened the heart of one woman—the first European convert to Christianity—and she in turn opened her house to Paul's missionary team. Notice that Lydia's conversion was part of *household* salvation:

> *And when she was baptized, and her household,*
> *she besought us, saying, If ye have judged me to*
> *be faithful to the Lord, come into my house, and*
> *abide there. And she constrained us* (Acts 16:15).

Paul's second convert in Europe was a demon-possessed girl. So we turn from Lydia, a cultured lady, a business woman, to a captive slave, a demon-possessed girl. The gospel can make a difference in *every* person's life. The girl had a spirit of *divination*, which is translated from the Greek word *python*, meaning a huge serpent. This demon-possessed girl made so-called inspired utterances. Those who owned her used her to tell fortunes. She was a very valuable piece of property to them, and she was entirely at their mercy. This was a pitiful, pitiful sight.

She followed Paul and his company, crying out after them. She called them servants of the most high God. Paul didn't minister to her right away; he waited awhile and then cast the spirits out of her. The girl was instantly set free—her soul was free! But she had no ability now to give evil prophecies or to tell fortunes, and her masters were furious.

Only twice in the book of Acts are gentiles seen persecuting Paul and the Church, and both times the persecution arose over the issue of money. This time the girl's owners became irate when they saw that their livelihood had been taken from them:

> *And when her masters saw that the hope of their gains was gone, they caught Paul and Silas, and drew them into the marketplace unto the rulers* (Acts 16:19).

The apostles were terribly beaten:

> *And the multitude rose up together against them: and the magistrates rent off their clothes, and commanded to beat them. And when they had laid many stripes upon them, they cast them into prison, . . . and made their feet fast in the stocks* (Acts 16:23-25).

THE PHILIPPIAN JAILER BELIEVES

Despite their stripes and stocks, Paul and Silas were preachers in prison at midnight. Singing and praising God, they had songs in the night. The prisoners heard them, and there was deliverance for all! God sent a very *intelligent* earthquake—it didn't kill anyone, it just shook up the place and loosened the chains of the prisoners and the doors of the prisons.

Three miracles happened here: Paul and Silas were rejoicing in their suffering; the earthquake came and every door opened and every chain was undone; and no prisoner ran off. If the prisoners had left, the jailer would have been killed by the Roman government. When he was awakened out of his sleep and saw the doors were opened, he was ready to kill himself.

Paul told the jailer not to commit suicide, and the man immediately wanted to be saved. He and his whole family came to Christ. The one who had given Paul and Silas their stripes now *washed* their stripes:

> *And he took them the same hour of the night, and washed their stripes; and was baptized, he and all his, straightway* (Acts 16:33).

It was just as though God was anointing Paul and Silas' heads in the presence of their enemies—their cup was overflowing.

I love Paul's boldness. He had certain legal rights as a Roman citizen, and he invoked them rather than simply leave town quietly when he was released:

> *But Paul said unto them, They have beaten us openly uncondemned, being Romans, and have cast us into prison; and now do they thrust us out privily? nay verily; but let them come themselves and fetch us out* (Acts 16:37).

When Paul was imprisoned in Rome, he wrote to the church which he began in Philippi. You would think that his memories of this town would be negative—the beating, the stocks, and the public humiliation. But the church in Philippi was born as a result of the miraculous, and the epistle to the Philippians is filled with joy and rejoicing!

After being brought out of prison, Paul and Silas brought comfort to the new local church which was in the house of Lydia:

> *And they went out of the prison, and entered into the house of Lydia: and when they had seen the brethren, they comforted them, and departed* (Acts 16:40).

Here again we see the supernatural: the believers in Philippi should have been comforting Paul and Silas after their ordeal; but instead, Paul and Silas were supernaturally strengthened to bring comfort and encouragement to the saints in Lydia's house.

Not one to lay around bathing his wounds, Paul departed from Philippi to find new souls who hadn't yet heard the gospel. Next stops: Thessalonica, Berea, Athens, and eventually Corinth, where Paul would spend 1½ years and write two vitally important New Testament letters to the church at Thessalonica.

CHAPTER NINE

Unknown Gods and Know-it-all Athenians—
Paul Enlightens the Intellectuals
(Acts 17)

Many Christians talk about Paul's three missionary journeys and his final trip to Rome. However, Paul may have taken other trips that are not recorded in the book of Acts. For example in Paul's letter to the Romans, he mentioned his desire to travel to Spain:

> *When therefore I have performed this, and have sealed to them this fruit, I will come by you into Spain* (Romans 15:28).

I believe Paul did make it to Spain; but, of course, we have no proof as far as the Bible is concerned. If Paul wrote his letter to the Romans around 57 A.D., that would still leave him a year of traveling before his first arrest mentioned in Acts 21 (refer to the chart on page 89). At any rate, Paul certainly was well-traveled and had a heart for spreading the gospel as far and as wide as possible!

In Acts 17 we see Paul on the road, passing through the two small towns of Amphipolis and Apollonia. His first destination was the largest population center and the chief seaport of Macedonia: Thessalonica (refer to the map on page 220). The city was founded by Cassander three centuries before and had been named after Cassander's wife, the sister of Alexander the Great.

As in every place he visited, Paul began preaching in the synagogue. Paul taught there for three sabbaths before being forced to leave. His stay in Thessalonica may have been longer than three weeks; perhaps he taught in private homes for almost six months. We know that Paul supported himself by making tents:

> *For ye remember, brethren, our labour and travail: for labouring night and day, because we would not be chargeable unto any of you, we preached unto you the gospel of God* (I Thessalonians 2:9).

A great multitude believed:

> *And some of them believed, and consorted with Paul and Silas; and of the devout Greeks a great multitude, and of the chief women not a few* (Acts 17:4).

These "devout Greeks" were Greek-speaking Jews. Paul was accepted because he was a well-schooled rabbi; Silas was from Jerusalem; and Timothy was a half-Jew and had been circumcised by Paul. They were all accepted at the beginning of their preaching. Paul mentioned the Thessalonians' openness in his first letter to them:

> *For this cause also thank we God without ceasing, because, when ye received the word of God which ye heard of us, ye received it not as the word of men, but as it is in truth, the word of God, which effectually worketh also in you that believe* (I Thessalonians 2:13).

REVIVALS AND RIOTS

But there was also opposition wherever Paul preached. It seemed that two things always followed Paul—revivals and riots. The envious Jews charged Paul with turning the world upside down, but it was really just the reverse. The unbelieving Jews were jealous of Paul's success in evangelizing the multitude. These Jews stirred up the crowds and stormed the house of Jason, where Paul and his company were staying. Jason was dragged before the authorities and accused of the charge of high treason because Paul supposedly had spoken against Caesar. However, the magistrate allowed Jason to go free after posting bail.

Paul was hurried away by night to Berea—some 60 miles

away. This was evidently the last time Paul was physically in Thessalonica:

> *Wherefore we would have come unto you, even I*
> *Paul, once and again; but Satan hindered us*
> (I Thessalonians 2:18).

As you study the books of Thessalonians, you'll find that although this church was subject to persecution, it stayed true to God. Because Paul was hindered from returning, he wrote two letters to them. Sometimes what seems like a failure can turn out to be a blessing. Satan's hindering resulted in two wonderful letters that still speak to millions today!

Both of the Thessalonian letters concentrate heavily on the Second Coming of Jesus. First Thessalonians deals with the coming of Christ as it affects the Church, and II Thessalonians is concerned with the coming of Christ as it affects the world.

Despite their treatment in Thessalonica, Paul, Silas, and Timothy went directly to the synagogue in Berea. The Jews there were very eager to study the Word. They were neither hardhearted, closed, prejudiced, or gullible. They searched the Word and many believed.

When the Jews from Thessalonica heard that Paul was preaching in Berea—and having success—they made the 60-mile trip by foot to stir up opposition once again. Imagine their hatred for Paul to make such a long trip on foot! The hatred of the Jews seemed primarily to be against Paul, not Silas and Timothy. Paul left Berea immediately, following the advice of Jesus:

> *But when they persecute you in this city, flee ye into another: . . .* (Matthew 10:23).

Silas and Timothy were able to remain in Berea while Paul set sail for Athens—the sophisticated, academic center of the world. This would be a whole new group of people, drastically different from the Greek Jews of Thessalonica and Berea.

DESPISE NOT PROPHESYING

I love the way God fulfills His calling upon believers' lives. Do you recall the prophecy Jesus spoke to Ananias when He wanted Ananias to pray for Saul (Paul)? In that prophecy the Lord summed up Paul's ministry:

> *But the Lord said unto him* [Ananias], *Go thy way: for he* [Paul] *is a chosen vessel unto me, to bear my name before the Gentiles, and kings, and the children of Israel* (Acts 9:15).

We have seen throughout the early part of Paul's ministry how he went into the synagogues to argue with the Jews concerning Jesus. Now, because of opposition from the Jews in Thessalonica, Paul traveled to Athens to speak before the

ACTS

gentiles there. God can turn around anything (including opposition to the gospel) and use it for good if we'll allow Him to guide and direct us. Later in the book of Acts, we'll see Paul travel to Jerusalem to speak to the Jewish leadership there; and we'll eventually see Paul stand before kings and rulers too. Ananias no doubt passed along Jesus' prophecy concerning Paul's ministry when he laid hands on him:

> *And hath seen in a vision a man named Ananias coming in, and putting his hand on him, that he might receive his sight* (Acts 9:12).

We should never limit God's Word or seek to have it fulfilled according to our preconceived ideas. The prophecy spoken over Paul's life literally was fulfilled in the book of Acts—but not always in the way Paul expected!

PAUL IN ATHENS

The Parthenon of Athens (the temple dedicated to the virgin Athena, the goddess of wisdom and the arts) was built on a hill (the Acropolis) and overlooked the whole city. Jerusalem was the religious center of that day; Rome the political center; but Athens was the architectural, cultural, and intellectual center.

Antioch, Tarsus, Ephesus, and Alexandria were also hubs of philosophic learning but nothing like Athens. Philosophers like Socrates, Plato, and Aristotle were centered at Athens.

152

It also was literally a center of idols—it is said that there were nearly 3,000 idols in the city of Athens!

The Greeks gave us much—a love of knowledge, a love of beauty, and a love of freedom. But spiritually, they were bankrupt. They would find many truths, but never THE TRUTH. They were involved with Greek mythology for 800 years and then with Greek philosophy for 500 years.

It was very clear to Paul that human wisdom was foolishness. The end result of man's knowledge only leads to streets lined with ridiculous idols. Paul surveyed the scene before him and must have been angry at Satan for blinding men's eyes and for keeping them in bondage.

As usual, Paul took his message to the synagogue first:

> *Therefore disputed he in the synagogue with the Jews, and with the devout persons, and in the market daily with them that met with him* (Acts 17:17).

Paul wasn't a tourist, he was a missionary. His preaching wasn't confined to the Jewish synagogue; he took his message to the "Agora" or central marketplace of Athens.

Verse 18 of this chapter requires some explanation:

> *Then certain philosophers of the Epicureans, and of the Stoicks, encountered him. And some said, What will this babbler say? other some, He seemeth*

to be a setter forth of strange gods: because he
preached unto them Jesus, and the resurrection
(Acts 17:18).

The Epicureans were of a certain school of philosophy that
had been founded by Epicurus (342-270 B.C.). They believed
that indulgence was the key to life. Our word "epicure" (a
person who has a fine taste for food and drink) is derived
from this philosophy.

The Epicureans felt that there were gods, but the gods
had no interest in mankind. Therefore man's chief end was
to seek pleasure in this life—because there was no
resurrection or life after death.

The Stoics were in many ways the opposite. They were
followers of a man named *Zeno* of Cyprus (340 to 260 B.C.).
Although they too denied any resurrection, their main
belief centered around living a life free of passion, joy, grief,
pain, or pleasure. Indifference was to be the key to life. They
were basically stern and impassive.

These two groups of philosophers came together to
confront Paul and his teaching. Some called Paul a
"babbler." The word "babbler" comes from the Greek word
"spermologos," a small bird that picks up seed along the
road. Paul was being called a "scrap-picker," someone who
just picked up this teaching and that but nothing that would
really appeal to an intelligent person.

Other Athenians sneered at the gospel and said that Paul
seemed to be a proclaimer of "strange gods." The word for

"gods" is *daimonion,* which is usually translated as "devil" or "demons." With such hostility to the gospel, it is no wonder that there was no substantial church established in Athens until 200 years after Paul's visit!

These intellectuals took Paul to Areopagus (a limestone hill between the Acropolis and the Agora) which was also known as Mars Hill. This was where the temple of Mars stood and the court of the Areopagus convened. This was a civil court which actually exercised a great deal of authority over people like Paul.

The Athenians were always open to some new kind of philosophy. They spent their leisure hours picking up bits of news, looking for new philosophies, and new "so-called" intellectual interests. We would say that *they* were the seed-pickers! Paul stood boldly and preached the gospel; he was a soul winner at heart. Let's take a close look at Paul's presentation to these intellectual Anthenians:

> *Then Paul stood in the midst of Mars' hill, and said, Ye men of Athens, I perceive that in all things ye are too superstitious* (Acts 17:22).

The Greek phrase "too superstitious" might be better translated "deeply religious" or "religiously disposed." Paul did not begin his sermon by insulting his listeners—he was more wise than that.

> *For as I passed by, and beheld your devotions, I found an altar with this inscription, TO THE*

155

UNKNOWN GOD. Whom therefore ye ignorantly worship, him declare I unto you (Acts 17:23).

Their "devotions" were actually the idols they worshiped. Paul called attention to the god that they worshiped called "Agnostos," the *unknown*. They knew everything that could be humanly known in that day, but they didn't know God. Jesus came to reveal God to man, and Paul had come to Athens to tell them about Jesus.

Always with the Jews, Paul reasoned out of the scriptures. But with these gentiles, he reasoned from creation:

> *God that made the world and all things therein, seeing that he is Lord of heaven and earth, dwelleth not in temples made with hands; Neither is worshipped with men's hands, as though he needed any thing, seeing he giveth to all life, and breath, and all things; And hath made of one blood all nations of men for to dwell on all the face of the earth, and hath determined the times before appointed, and the bounds of their habitation; That they should seek the Lord, if haply they might feel after him, and find him, though he be not far from every one of us* (Acts 17:24-27).

Paul's message was aimed at the incompatibility of idols with the very nature of God. Next Paul reminds them that idolatry is incompatible with the nature of man:

For in him we live, and move, and have our being;
as certain also of your own poets have said, For
we are also his offspring. Forasmuch then as we
are the offspring of God, we ought not to think that
the Godhead is like unto gold, or silver, or stone,
graven by art and man's device (Acts 17:28,29).

To these "know-it-alls" Paul now tightens down the screws and exposes their ignorance of God and His demands upon men:

And the times of this ignorance God winked at;
but now commandeth all men every where to
repent: Because he hath appointed a day, in the
which he will judge the world in righteousness
by that man whom he hath ordained; whereof he
hath given assurance unto all men, in that he
hath raised him from the dead (Acts 17:30,31).

Paul was quite comprehensive in his presentation of the true God—the God of creation, the source and sustainer of all life, the God of all mankind, the omnipresent God, the omnipotent God, the God Who is a Spirit, the God Who enlightens our ignorance and Who demands repentance because He is the judge of all.

THE HARDNESS
OF ATHENS

The resurrection, of course, is at the heart of our Christian faith; and Paul did not fail to seal his message with the fact of Jesus' resurrection. The resurrection of Jesus Christ is the guarantee of ours. The gospel, however, usually does not have its greatest impact on those who are wise after the flesh. No great church was founded in Athens during the first 200 years of Christianity; the gospel message first had to dislodge 1300 years of men's wisdom and men's idolatry!

But neither was Paul's sermon in vain, by any means. There was a distinguished member of the Athenian court who was converted (Dionysius the Areopagite), as well as one Damaris, "and others with them" (Acts 17:34).

I think Paul's experience in Athens stuck with him for some time. Later he would write:

> For it is written, I will destroy the wisdom of the wise, and will bring to nothing the understanding of the prudent. Where is the wise? where is the scribe? where is the disputer of this world? hath not God made foolish the wisdom of this world? For after that in the wisdom of God the world by wisdom knew not God, it pleased God by the foolishness of preaching to save them that believe. For the Jews require a sign, and the Greeks seek after wisdom: But we preach Christ crucified, unto the Jews a stumblingblock, and unto the Greeks foolishness; But unto them which are called, both Jews and Greeks, Christ the power of God, and the wisdom of God (I Corinthians 1:19-24).

Athens would eventually become a strong Christian center, but for now Paul would push on to the city whose very name became a synonym for licentiousness: Corinth. Here Paul would stay for 1½ years and build a thriving, if somewhat immature, church. Rather than approach his listeners from an intellectual viewpoint in Corinth, Paul's preaching would be "*. . . not with enticing words of man's wisdom, but in demonstration of the Spirit and of power*" (I Corinthians 2:4).

CHAPTER TEN

Corruption at Corinth— Paul Confronts Immorality and Solidifies the Churches
(Acts 18-21:17)

Leaving the intellectual snobbery of Athens, Paul traveled 46 miles to preach the gospel in quite a different setting—a first-century navy town which eventually became a synonym for licentiousness! Corinth was the political capital of Greece during Paul's day. Sea routes and land routes came together at Corinth, making it a commercial and trade center between Italy and all of Asia. (Refer to the map on page 221 for locations mentioned in this chapter.)

The temple of Venus was located in Corinth. Its more than one thousand male and female prostitutes added to the city's blatant corruption. Imagine Paul walking into a city of 500,000 people who were actually proud of their reputation for looseness. Paul was certainly not one to be intimidated; he knew that the gospel was " . . . *the power of God unto salvation to every one that believeth; . . .* " (Romans 1:16).

At Corinth Paul met Aquila and Priscilla, who were tentmakers as was Paul. Aquila and Priscilla had been affected by the persecution against all Jews in Rome. The Jews, naturally, were appalled by the idolatry of the Romans. The Romans, in turn, were jealous of the Jewish diligence in areas of commerce, education, and government. Around 51 A.D. Rome expelled all Jews, which God used for His purposes by bringing Aquila and Priscilla into contact with Paul:

> *After these things Paul departed from Athens, and came to Corinth; And found a certain Jew named Aquila, born in Pontus, lately come from Italy, with his wife Priscilla; (because that Claudius had commanded all Jews to depart from Rome:) and come unto them* (Acts 18:1,2).

Paul labored in trade with them:

> *And labour, working with our own hands: being reviled, we bless; being persecuted, we suffer it* (I Corinthians 4:12).

> *For ye remember, brethren, our labour and travail: for labouring night and day, because we would not be chargeable unto any of you, we preached unto you the gospel of God* (I Thessalonians 2:9).

Paul was a tentmaker by trade, but he was also building the tabernacle of the Lord at Corinth. Tentmaking enabled

Paul to give himself to missionary work. According to his custom, Paul used the Jewish synagogue as his forum:

And he reasoned in the synagogue every sabbath, and persuaded the Jews and the Greeks (Acts 18:4).

Another custom that Paul seemed to have was stirring up opposition. The Jews couldn't argue against Paul's message so they finally "blasphemed" and forced Paul to declare, "*. . . Your blood be upon your own heads; I am clean: from henceforth I will go unto the Gentiles*" (Acts 18:6).

However, Paul didn't go far from the synagogue! He found an open door in the house of Justus, whose house was actually *attached* to the synagogue. Imagine the anger of the Jews in that part of town when their own chief ruler, Crispus, believed Paul's message and received Jesus as "the Christ"! Crispus was one of the few Corinthians personally baptized by Paul:

I thank God that I baptized none of you, but Crispus and Gaius (I Corinthians 1:14).

All of Crispus' house were saved and baptized. Then the Lord gave Paul a vision, telling him that He had many people in the city of Corinth. The vision strengthened and encouraged Paul.

Corinth was a ripened harvest field. Paul had seen very little success in preaching the gospel in Athens. But in Corinth there were many hungry hearts; consequently, Paul stayed in Corinth for a year and a half. Paul entered into a different phase of his missionary ministry. Before he seemed to go at a fast pace from place to place. But now, in the next five years, he would be centered between two cities—Corinth on the European mainland and Ephesus in Asia.

When a new proconsul, Gallio, was appointed in Corinth, the Jews evidently thought it was the right time to accuse Paul before the town judgment seat. Their tactic didn't work. Gallio dismissed the matter and told the Jews to solve their differences amongst themselves.

The mob grabbed Sosthenes, the newly appointed chief leader of the synagogue, and beat him (probably because he was at least sympathetic toward Paul). Gallio saw the beating yet he didn't stop it. Perhaps this was the same Sosthenes mentioned by Paul in his letter to the Corinthians:

> *Paul, called to be an apostle of Jesus Christ through the will of God, and Sosthenes our brother* (I Corinthians 1:1).

MINISTRY AT EPHESUS

The time finally came for Paul to leave Corinth. He took Aquila and Priscilla with him and headed off for Ephesus, a flourishing city in Asia Minor. The route to Ephesus included a stop in the port city of Cenchrea where we're told that Paul got a hair cut which ended a vow taken earlier.

In the Old Testament the Nazarite vow forbid partaking of the fruit of the vine, touching a dead body, and cutting the hair. Perhaps this vow was part of Paul's tremendous burden for the Jews:

> *I say the truth in Christ, I lie not, my conscience also bearing me witness in the Holy Ghost, That I have great heaviness and continual sorrow in my heart. For I could wish that myself were accursed from Christ for my brethren, my kinsmen according to the flesh* (Romans 9:1-3).

> *Brethren, my heart's desire and prayer to God for Israel is, that they might be saved* (Romans 10:1).

The time of this Nazarite vow had expired so Paul cut his hair at Cenchrea before sailing for Ephesus, a very important commercial city in Asia Minor. Its chief pride was the temple of Diana or Artemis, which was one of the seven wonders of the ancient world. Shrewd Greek traders engaged in business relating to the idolatrous worship and magical art connected with the temple.

Again, Paul went to the synagogue and lost no time in presenting Jesus to the Jews. He did not, however, stay long in Ephesus at this time; he must have had great faith in Aquila and Priscilla to leave them in Ephesus after so little personal time there. Paul stopped briefly at Caesarea, saluted the church in Jerusalem, and finally returned to Antioch.

Undoubtedly Paul shared with his home church the victories of the harvest. He probably did not stay more than three months at Antioch, the place from which the church had originally sent him forth. Paul's mind was always on the mission field. On his second missionary journey, Paul had established New Testament local churches at Philippi, Thessalonica, Berea, Athens, and Corinth. The epistles to these churches give us tremendous revelation truth of Christ.

PAUL'S THIRD JOURNEY FOR JESUS

Aquila and Priscilla had stayed in Ephesus, teaching and strengthening the new believers. The Lord sent them a helper named Apollos, a very strong believer and a very strong preacher. Apollos was from Alexandria in Egypt. This city was the second largest of the Roman Empire. There was a large Jewish colony there; and in New Testament times, one third of the population of the city was made up of Jews. The Greek Septuagint version of the Bible was translated there.

One mark of any man or woman of God is teachability. Evidently Apollos had just that very quality! Aquila and Priscilla helped him become more knowledgeable in the Scriptures. Later they sent Apollos off with a written recommendation. He was well received by the new Christians wherever he went:

> And when he [Apollos] *was disposed to pass into Achaia, the brethren wrote, exhorting the disciples to receive him: who, when he was come, helped them much which had believed through grace: For he mightily convinced the Jews, and that*

*publickly, shewing by the scriptures that Jesus
was Christ* (Acts 18:27,28).

When Paul returned to Ephesus during his third
missionary trip, he met other believers whose understanding
of Christianity was limited. They knew of the baptism of
John, but not of the baptism of the Holy Spirit. They had
been baptized in water and evidently had received the
Lord Jesus as their Savior. Paul laid hands on them, and they
spoke with tongues and prophesied.

Paul went back into the Ephesian synagogue and for three
months taught them the Word of God, emphasizing the
kingdom. The kingdom was centered upon the King, Who
had been crucified at Calvary. The response from the Jews
was typical of past experiences:

> *But the unbelieving Jews stirred up the Gentiles,
> and made their minds evil affected against the
> brethren* (Acts 14:2).

> *But the Jews which believed not, moved with envy,
> took unto them certain lewd fellows of the baser
> sort, and gathered a company, and set all the city
> on an uproar, and assaulted the house of Jason,
> and sought to bring them out to the people*
> (Acts 17:5).

> *But when divers were hardened, and believed not,
> but spake evil of that way before the multitude,
> he departed from them, and separated the*

disciples, disputing daily in the school of one Tyrannus (Acts 19:9).

Tyrannus was a well-known teacher of the area; he probably had some type of "divinity" school. It has been suggested that Paul used the "school" building of Tyrannus from 11:00 a.m. until 2:00 in the afternoon, during the heat of the day when Tyrannus would not be using the building. So people would come to hear the Word of God during siesta times.

Paul spent two years teaching the believers in Ephesus, and God validated his authority by performing special miracles:

And God wrought special miracles by the hands of Paul: So that from his body were brought unto the sick handkerchiefs or aprons, and the diseases departed from them, and the evil spirits went out of them (Acts 19:11,12).

God can use all kinds of things to show His grace and healing power. He used a brazen serpent, the passover lamb, the waters of Jordan, the anointing oil—all to show forth His healing power. The "handkerchiefs or aprons" were points of contact and certainly nothing to be worshiped. You remember that Hezekiah had to destroy the brazen serpent which God had used for healing because the Jews had begun to worship it:

He removed the high places, and brake the images, and cut down the groves, and brake in pieces the

brasen serpent that Moses had made: for unto
those days the children of Israel did burn incense
to it: and he called it Nehushtan (II Kings 18:4).

REVIVAL AT EPHESUS

"Chief of the priests" in Acts 19:14 is the term normally used for the high priest and members of the Sanhedrin. If a town had 120 or more Jews, it had a local Sanhedrin of 23 members. If any town had fewer than this, they had at least 3 members on the Sanhedrin. Sceva probably was a member of the local Jewish Sanhedrin. His sons claimed special knowledge in casting out demons. The demons knew Jesus, but the demons didn't know Sceva's sons. So they turned and attacked them because demons have great strength:

And the man in whom the evil spirit was leaped
on them, and overcame them, and prevailed
against them, so that they fled out of that house
naked and wounded (Acts 19:16).

As the name of the Lord Jesus was magnified, the people were stirred up to renounce any past involvement in the occult. All kinds of books of magic and charms and curios used for spells were burned. These items were priced at 50,000 pieces of silver—enough money to buy an army of slaves. Jesus was sold for 30 pieces of silver, and He came to set the captives free.

After two years in Ephesus, Paul planned to go into

Macedonia and Achaia; and he sent some of his men ahead. Timothy was one of those men. When he had returned from Macedonia, he rejoined Paul at Corinth. Timothy seems to have run another errand for Paul to Corinth:

> *For this cause have I sent unto you Timotheus, who is my beloved son, and faithful in the Lord, who shall bring you into remembrance of my ways which be in Christ, as I teach every where in every church* (I Corinthians 4:17).

> *Now if Timotheus come, see that he may be with you without fear: for he worketh the work of the Lord, as I also do. Let no man therefore despise him: but conduct him forth in peace, that he may come unto me: for I look for him with the brethren* (I Corinthians 16:10,11).

The other man sent ahead to Macedonia was Erastus, who could have been at one time the treasurer of the city of Corinth:

> *Gaius mine host, and of the whole church, saluteth you. Erastus the chamberlain of the city saluteth you, and Quartus a brother* (Romans 16:23).

During this time it was not the Jews who became stirred up—it was the gentiles. With gentiles it was not a matter of doctrine; it was a matter of money. Their wealth was derived from making silver miniatures of the temple of Diana. Diana of the Ephesians was an obscenity—a gross image with licentious rites. She had been the ancient goddess of Asia Minor called Artemis.

Some of the tradesmen were concerned that they were going to become bankrupt if the number of Paul's converts kept increasing. A terrible riot broke out, and it was difficult to argue with a mob that was blinded with passion. Two of Paul's helpers, Gaius of Derbe and Aristarchus of Thessalonica, were recognized and seized. Eventually the mob was dispersed by the town clerk.

TOURING MACEDONIA AND GREECE

After the "uproar" was over, Paul departed for Macedonia where he no doubt visited churches in Philippi, Thessalonica, and Berea. From there he traveled into Greece, visiting churches in Athens, Corinth, and Cenchrea. It only took three months in Greece to stir up opposition again from the Jews. Paul had a quick change of plans when he learned of the Jews lying in wait for him. Leaving Philippi, Paul sailed to Troas where he preached and held the Lord's Supper on Sunday:

> *And upon the first day of the week, when the disciples came together to break bread, Paul preached unto them, ready to depart on the morrow; and continued his speech until midnight* (Acts 20:7).

Though the early Church kept the first day of the week,

we also see them keeping the feasts of the Passover and Unleavened Bread. This was a transition period—coming from the Old Covenant into the fullness of the New Covenant. The feast days had been so extremely important to the Jews, but Paul said:

> *Blotting out the handwriting of ordinances that was against us, which was contrary to us, and took it out of the way, nailing it to his cross; And having spoiled principalities and powers, he made a shew of them openly, triumphing over them in it. Let no man therefore judge you in meat, or in drink, or in respect of an holyday, or of the new moon, or of the sabbath days* (Colossians 2:14-16).

> *One man esteemeth one day above another: another esteemeth every day alike. Let every man be fully persuaded in his own mind. He that regardeth the day, regardeth it unto the Lord; and he that regardeth not the day, to the Lord he doth not regard it. He that eateth, eateth to the Lord, for he giveth God thanks; and he that eateth not, to the Lord he eateth not, and giveth God thanks. For none of us liveth to himself, and no man dieth to himself* (Romans 14:5-7).

The true sabbath is the rest in Christ and the baptism of the Holy Spirit:

> *But if I cast out devils by the Spirit of God, then the kingdom of God is come unto you. Or else how*

*can one enter into a strong man's house, and spoil
his goods, except he first bind the strong man? and
then he will spoil his house. He that is not with
me is against me; and he that gathereth not with
me scattereth abroad* (Matthew 12:28-30).

*There remaineth therefore a rest to the people of
God* (Hebrews 4:9).

*For precept must be upon precept, precept upon
precept; line upon line, line upon line; here a
little, and there a little: For with stammering
lips and another tongue will he speak to this
people. To whom he said, This is the rest
wherewith ye may cause the weary to rest; and
this is the refreshing: yet they would not hear*
(Isaiah 28:10-12).

The old sabbath, the seventh day of the week, was a sign
for the *nation of Israel*:

*Wherefore the children of Israel shall keep the
sabbath, to observe the sabbath throughout their
generations, for a perpetual covenant. It is a sign
between me and the children of Israel for ever: for
in six days the LORD made heaven and earth,
and on the seventh day he rested, and was
refreshed* (Exodus 31:16,17).

*Moreover also I gave them my sabbaths, to be a
sign between me and them, that they might*

173

know that I am the LORD that sanctify them (Ezekiel 20:12).

The New Covenant had a new day on which to worship. The early Church broke bread on the first day of the week:

And upon the first day of the week, when the disciples came together to break bread, Paul preached unto them, ready to depart on the morrow; and continued his speech until midnight (Acts 20:7).

They laid aside their collections on the first day of the week:

Upon the first day of the week let every one of you lay by him in store, as God hath prospered him, that there be no gatherings when I come (I Corinthians 16:2).

Jesus arose on the first day of the week; the Holy Spirit was poured out at Pentecost on the first day of the week. It's not hard to see why the Jews hated Paul; he preached about, wrote about, and personally celebrated a "new sabbath" that would have infuriated the followers of Moses.

In less than 16 years, Paul had evangelized 15,000 square miles. Now at Troas Paul again broke bread with the disciples and preached a lengthy sermon. Paul continued his preaching until very late. The upper room was three stories up, and we know from the story that a young man fell out of the window to his death. But through Paul he

was raised from the dead. Both Elijah and Elisha had similar
miracles in their ministry:

> And he stretched himself upon the child three
> times, and cried unto the LORD, and said, O LORD
> my God, I pray thee, let this child's soul come into
> him again (I Kings 17:21).

> And he went up, and lay upon the child, and put
> his mouth upon his mouth, and his eyes upon
> his eyes, and his hands upon his hands: and he
> stretched himself upon the child; and the flesh
> of the child waxed warm (II Kings 4:34).

MINISTRY ON THE WAY TO JERUSALEM

Paul walked the 20 miles to Assos while the others in his
party went by ship. Paul probably wanted the time alone.

After a number of quick stops along the coast, Paul
arrived at Miletus where he sent a messenger to Ephesus
to call a meeting of the elders of that church. They walked
the 30 miles from Ephesus to Miletus to hear a final
message from the great apostle. Paul charged them to
" . . . feed the church of God, which he hath purchased
with his own blood" (Acts 20:28).

Chapter 21 begins Paul's ministry at Tyre. This is an
ancient Phoenician city, but it had a church there which
was established after the persecution of Stephen:

Now they which were scattered abroad upon the persecution that arose about Stephen travelled as far as Phenice, and Cyprus, and Antioch, preaching the word to none but unto the Jews only (Acts 11:19).

Paul was warned of the danger awaiting him in Jerusalem, but that did not deter him from following God's leading in his spirit. From Tyre, Paul and his group went to Ptolemais and then on to Caesarea where they lodged with Philip the evangelist. He was one of the seven original deacons of the Jerusalem church. He took the gospel to the Samaritans and was used mightily.

Philip had four daughters who were prophetesses. However, they did not minister the word of prophecy to Paul. Instead it was Agabus, the same prophet who had prophesied the wide-spread famine that would affect the world:

And in these days came prophets from Jerusalem unto Antioch. And there stood up one of them named Agabus, and signified by the Spirit that there should be great dearth throughout all the world: which came to pass in the days of Claudius Caesar (Acts 11:27,28).

Agabus gave Paul his last warning about the suffering awaiting him if he went to Jerusalem. Paul knew in his spirit that bonds and imprisonment were awaiting him:

And now, behold I go bound in the spirit unto

*Jerusalem, not knowing the things that shall befall
me there: Save that the Holy Ghost witnesseth in
every city, saying that bonds and afflictions abide
me* (Acts 20:22-24).

Paul also knew in his spirit that he would go to Rome:

*After these things were ended, Paul purposed in
the spirit, when he had passed through Macedonia
and Achaia to go to Jerusalem, saying, After I
have been there, I must also see Rome. So he sent
into Macedonia two of them that ministered unto
him, Timotheus and Erastus; but he himself
stayed in Asia for a season* (Acts 19:21,22).

Paul knew that he was to go, and he also knew the
afflictions which awaited him. He knew God's will, even
though his witness would not be accepted:

*And it came to pass, that, when I was come again
to Jerusalem, even while I prayed in the temple,
I was in a trance; And saw him saying unto me,
Make haste, and get thee quickly out of Jerusalem:
for they will not receive thy testimony concerning
me* (Acts 22:17,18).

*And the night following the Lord stood by him,
and said, Be of good cheer, Paul: for as thou hast
testified of me in Jerusalem, so must thou bear
witness also at Rome* (Acts 23:11).

When the brethren could not persuade Paul to give up

his plans, they simply said to him, "The will of the Lord be done." Paul knew the will of God, and he purposed in his heart to obey the Lord's leading.

It was 65 miles from Caesarea to Jerusalem. When Paul arrived in Jerusalem, he was gladly received by the brethren. Their joy (Paul's and the brethren in Jerusalem) would be short-lived. In a little over one week, Paul would be beaten by the Jews and arrested by the gentiles—just the beginning of his long trip to Rome and the suffering which the Holy Spirit had shown him was to come.

CHAPTER ELEVEN

Under Arrest!— Dangerous Times for Paul
(Acts 21:18-23:35)

Eight years following the Jerusalem Council, we see the church at Jerusalem still living a double life of law and grace. This predominantly Jewish group of believers was still under the strong influence of Judaism. We can thank God for Paul's clear vision of salvation through faith alone. He was certainly God's man-of-the-hour for the Church. Paul's spoken and written words are absolutely the inspired foundation of the Christian faith.

Paul took his missions' report to James and all the elders of the church in Jerusalem. James was the bishop of the Jerusalem church. The elders must have felt a bit uneasy with Paul's detailed accounts of gentile salvation. Yes, they "glorified the Lord" (Acts 21:20) when Paul finished his report; but they had something on their minds which overshadowed God's working among the gentiles:

. . . Thou seest, brother, how many thousands of

Jews there are which believe; and they are all zealous of the law: And they are informed of thee, that thou teachest all the Jews which are among the Gentiles to forsake Moses, saying that they ought not to circumcise their children, neither to walk after the customs (Acts 21:20,21).

The elders still thought that being a good Christian meant being a good Jew. They were eager to prove to the Jewish believers in Jerusalem that Paul was still a good Jew as well as a Christian. Paul was known for being a troublemaker; riots followed him wherever he went. To avoid trouble, the elders had already thought of what Paul could do to pacify the multitudes gathered in Jerusalem for the Passover Feast:

Do therefore this that we say to thee: We have four men which have a vow on them; Them take, and purify thyself with them, and be at charges with them, that they may shave their heads: and all may know that those things whereof they were informed concerning thee, are nothing; but that thou thyself also walkest orderly, and keepest the law (Acts 21:23,24).

Paul was well aware that Mosaic rituals, the Aaronic priesthood, sacrifices, and oblations, were abolished in Jesus Christ. Paul was well aware of the veil which was torn in two. Soon God would make it impossible to keep most of these rituals; Jerusalem, with its Temple, would be leveled by the Roman prince Titus in 70 A.D. In the meantime, the Christians were living in a transition period from the Old Covenant to the New Covenant.

PAUL TAKES A VOW

If anyone knew grace, it was Paul; but he agreed to go along with the elders' suggestion. He was following the words which he had already written in his letter to the Corinthians:

> ... I am made all things to all men, that I might by all means save some (I Corinthians 9:22).

Paul accompanied the four men into the Temple. When the Jews from Asia saw Paul in the Temple, they were extremely angry. Paul had had a very fruitful ministry in Asia, especially in Ephesus; and for this the Jews hated him. They were angry because they thought that Paul had brought Trophimus, a gentile, into the sacred area of the Temple reserved for Jews only. Their Temple was being defiled by a gentile—or so they thought.

Luke says that the whole city was in an uproar over the rumor spread about Paul. The people dragged Paul out of the inner court of the Temple. They had every intention of killing him! Paul could have been torn to pieces by the mob if the commander of the Roman garrison hadn't arrived with his men. They saved Paul's life by taking him into custody and handcuffing him. Paul's "career" as a prisoner had now begun.

The mob cried, "Away with him." This had been screamed 27 years before into the ears of Pilate:

And they cried out all at once, saying, Away with this man, and release unto us Barabbas (Luke 23:18).

But they cried out, Away with him, away with him, crucify him. Pilate saith unto them, Shall I crucify your King? The chief priests answered, We have no king but Caesar (John 19:15).

PAUL BEFORE THE MOB

Paul never missed an opportunity to preach the gospel. He addressed the chief captain who was surprised that Paul spoke Greek. Paul asked for permission to speak to the mob; and as he spoke to them in Hebrew, he gained their attention.

Now we see the prophetic Word of the Lord to Ananias being fulfilled:

. . . Go thy way: for he is a chosen vessel unto me, to bear my name before the Gentiles, and kings, and the children of Israel: For I will shew him how great things he must suffer for my name's sake (Acts 9:15,16).

We see Paul before the gentiles in Acts 14-20, before kings in Acts 24-26, and before the children of Israel in Acts 22,23.

Paul shared his testimony with the crowd of Jews from his conversion on the road to Damascus, the part Ananias had played in restoring his sight, and the vision he had received while in the Temple.

When Paul mentioned the gentiles, the Jews went into a rage. Were it not for the chief captain ordering Paul to be brought into the Roman headquarters, he would have been killed. But Paul's fate at the hands of the Romans was not to be much better; the chief captain ordered him to be scourged. Scourging could be fatal. The whip had leather straps inlaid with little pieces of iron. When a man was beaten, it would tear out his flesh. If one thong hit a man's face, it could blind him.

Paul mentioned his beatings in II Corinthians 11:24. He had suffered flogging five times from the Jews. Still, Paul rejoiced in his sufferings:

Who now rejoice in my sufferings for you, and fill up that which is behind of the afflictions of Christ in my flesh for his body's sake, which is the church (Colossians 1:24).

Paul "rejoiced" in his sufferings, but he by no means *volunteered* for beatings. Claiming his civil rights as a Roman citizen entitled to a trial, Paul was delivered from the scourging.

PAUL BEFORE THE SANHEDRIN

Once again Paul had the opportunity to witness before the Jews—this time the Sanhedrin. After Paul spoke only one sentence in his defense, the high priest ordered him to be struck on the mouth. We get a good glimpse of Paul's temper in his reply to the high priest:

> *Then said Paul unto him, God shall smite thee, thou whited wall: for sittest thou to judge me after the law, and commandest me to be smitten contrary to the law?* (Acts 23:3).

Paul called him a "whited wall." Jesus, in Matthew 23:27, had called the Pharisees and Scribes, "whited sepulchers." These sepulchers were white-washed at the time of Passover so that no one would be ceremonially defiled and hindered from keeping the feast. They were full of dead men's bones and rottenness. They were "white-washed," but not "washed white."

Paul was charged with reviling God's high priest, and Paul admitted that he was wrong to speak in such a manner. Paul's apology is quoted from Exodus:

> *Thou shalt not revile the gods, nor curse the ruler of thy people* (Exodus 22:28).

The wisdom of God gave Paul the strategy he needed to

use on the Pharisees and the Sadducees. Paul had been raised a Pharisee:

> *Circumcised the eighth day, of the stock of Israel, of the tribe of Benjamin, an Hebrew of the Hebrews; as touching the law, a Pharisee* (Philippians 3:5).

It was easier for Pharisees to become Christians than it was for Sadducees because Sadducees denied the miraculous and the Resurrection. So Paul tossed a high explosive into the Council. Paul said that he was a Pharisee being accused by Sadducees. The two parties went at each other's throats. Basically, it was liberals against conservatives. The Pharisees demanded that Paul be set free. The Sadducees refused. Each group began to pull at Paul until finally the Romans had to step in and take Paul into custody. They literally rescued Paul from death once again.

The Lord visited and encouraged Paul as He had on two previous occasions:

> *Then spake the Lord to Paul in the night by a vision, Be not afraid, but speak, and hold not thy peace* (Acts 18:9).

> *And it came to pass, that when I was come again to Jerusalem, even while I prayed in the temple, I was in a trance* (Acts 22:17).

> *And the night following the Lord stood by him, and said, Be of good cheer, Paul: for as thou hast*

testified of me in Jerusalem, so must thou bear
witness also at Rome (Acts 23:11).

It was time for Paul to begin witnessing in a whole new field of ministry. Now the radicals of both parties got together and decided that it was time to kill Paul. They took an oath upon themselves; they said they would go on a hunger strike until they had killed Paul. It looks like they starved to death because they never got that opportunity.

The plot to kill Paul was overheard by Paul's nephew and eventually related to the chief captain. Once again God used the Romans to save Paul's life and to deliver him safely to another government official. The Lord was setting up another opportunity for Paul to share his testimony.

It seems like the sovereignty of God is seen in little things. In the case of Daniel, a king couldn't understand a dream; in the case of Joseph, two dreams were given to a pharaoh; in the case of Moses, a young princess fell in love with a baby; in the case of Esther, the king spent a sleepless night. Each incident was a little hinge upon which a large door of opportunity swung in favor of God's people. Truly God is at work in *every* circumstance and situation of life.

Paul was taken to Caesarea by an escort of 472 Roman soldiers! There he would stay in limbo for two years as a prisoner. Through it all Paul would maintain the proper attitude. He knew all along that he was really a "prisoner of Jesus Christ" (Philemon 1).

CHAPTER TWELVE

Judgment Upon the Judges—Three Who Said "No" to the Savior
(Acts 24-26)

Wouldn't you be excited if you knew that God wanted you to speak before kings and rulers? If you weren't careful, it might be easy to become a bit boastful and proud! God told Ananias that Paul would bear His name before "... *Gentiles, and kings, and the children of Israel*" (Acts 9:15). But little did Paul know at that time what the conditions would be when he finally stood before the rulers of his day—as a prisoner of the state. No room for any pride there! Chapters 24-26 of Acts give a good look at the fulfillment of this prophecy in Paul's life. We see the apostle bearing the name of Jesus before governors Felix and Festus and before King Agrippa. Sadly, there is no record of them receiving Paul's witness.

It may be that Luke was using a bit of sarcasm when he wrote about the *high* priest *descending* with the elders to Caesarea. They brought a smooth talker named Tertullus with them, and they probably thought they had their case all wrapped up. Tertullus was a flatterer and a liar. Let's look at the charges which were brought against Paul (Acts 24:5,6):

1. He was a pestilent fellow.

2. He was a mover of sedition.

3. He was the ringleader of the sect of the Nazarenes.

4. He profaned the Temple.

Evidently the Jews had decided not to call Paul a "Christian" but rather a "Nazarene." The Galilean town of Nazareth was a despised town:

> *And Nathanael said unto him, Can there any good thing come out of Nazareth?* . . . (John 1:46).

> *They answered and said unto him, Art thou also of Galilee? Search, and look: for out of Galilee ariseth no prophet* (John 7:52).

However, it was Jonah, the only prophet to whom Jesus directly likened Himself, who came from Gath-hepher, which is only three miles northeast of Nazareth!

The following is Paul's defense before Felix against the false accusations (verses 10-21):

1. Paul had not been found in the Temple "disputing with any man."

2. Paul had not been "raising up the people" in the synagogues or anywhere in the city.

3. The Jews could present no proof for any of their charges.

4. Paul brought in his witness about the Lord Jesus Christ.

5. Paul told of his hope of the resurrection of the just.

6. Paul testified that he went to Jerusalem, taking alms and offerings to the people.

7. Paul said he was fulfilling a vow of purification; it was Jews from Asia who caused the problem.

8. There were no Asian Jews there to give any evidence.

9. The only disruption caused by Paul was when he alleged that he was on trial before the Sanhedrin because of his belief in the resurrection.

It appears that Felix knew more than the Jews about the sect of the Nazarene. He deferred Paul's case until the chief captain Lysias came down from Jerusalem to give further evidence. Paul was kept in custody, but his friends were allowed to visit him. Paul was given every consideration as a Roman citizen. Of course Felix knew that Ananias and his crowd were scoundrels and liars—just like he was.

There were no Christians from Jerusalem who went to help Paul with his testimony or to stand with him. It seems strange that the Christian community at Jerusalem did nothing to help him.

Days later Felix brought his wife Drusilla to hear Paul. Drusilla was a Jewess. She was the youngest daughter of Herod Agrippa I. This is the Herod who murdered James and would have murdered Peter (Acts 12:1-3).

Paul, as he sat before Drusilla and Felix, strongly preached righteousness, temperance, and of the judgment to come. Paul called them to repentance before judgment, giving them an escape through Jesus. There is no question that Felix was dealt with by the Holy Spirit, for Paul's words were like sharp swords into Felix's conscience. Felix trembled, he was terrified, he was convicted. But it looks like cash was on his mind more than Christ; verse 26 tells us that Felix was hoping for a bribe from Paul. How sad! Though Paul preached of righteousness, Felix wanted Paul to be *unrighteous* in offering a bribe.

Festus Hears the Gospel

Two years went by after which there was a civil war between the Jews and gentiles at Caesarea. Felix took troops and stopped the war, using great violence against the Jews. Rome called Felix back and demanded an account of his behavior. Paul was handed over to Procius Festus, the new procurator.

The new governor couldn't have cared less about Paul. He merely wanted favor with the Jews under his charge so he left Paul imprisoned. Festus went to Jerusalem and faced the Sanhedrin. The Jews were very clever, and Festus certainly wanted to get along with them.

The Jewish leadership put much pressure on Festus to get Paul released from Caesarea and back to trial in Jerusalem. But God holds the hearts of men in His hands, and Festus didn't give in to the Jew's request. God overrode the Jewish leadership.

After ten days Festus returned to Caesarea and brought Paul before the judgment seat. It must have been a terribly frustrating time for Paul—to have to appear before Festus when he had already appeared before Felix, who knew he was innocent. Festus knew less about Jewish law, and it would be even more difficult for Paul to defend himself. But Paul's faith was not in man's knowledge; it was in God.

The Jews came down with their same complaints. Then they added some charges against Paul concerning Caesar. Luke summarizes Paul's defense:

> *While he answered for himself, Neither against the law of the Jews, neither against the temple, nor yet against Caesar, have I offended any thing at all* (Acts 25:8).

Paul took a strong stand for Christian obedience to governing powers. Earlier he had written to the Christians living in Rome:

Let every soul be subject unto the higher powers.
For there is no power but of God: the powers that
be are ordained of God. Whosoever therefore
resisteth the power, resisteth the ordinance of God:
and they that resist shall receive to themselves
damnation. For rulers are not a terror to good
works, but to the evil. Wilt thou then not be afraid
of the power? do that which is good, and thou shalt
have praise of the same (Romans 13:1-3).

Festus asked Paul whether he would like to go to Jerusalem to be judged. Paul, knowing that he must bear witness in Rome, exercised his Roman citizenship and appealed to Caesar. Festus conferred with his private council and agreed to send Paul to Rome.

Agrippa Hears the Gospel

In the meantime King Agrippa and his wife came to Caesarea to pay their respects to the new governor. Agrippa was well acquainted with Jewish law, and after some days Festus spoke to him about Paul's case.

What beautiful opportunities Felix and Festus had, and how blinded they were. Jesus knocked at the doors of their hearts, and they didn't bother to go to the door. We can trace the Lord's hand of mercy appearing before the Herods for many generations. Herod the Great had the wise men come to him looking for a king. He searched the Scriptures, but missed the King of all kings and had the babies at Bethlehem murdered.

His son, Herod Antipas, had John the Baptist beheaded. King Herod Agrippa I killed the apostle James and intended to murder Peter, but Peter was rescued. Each one of these men saw the miraculous and refused it. The last Herod heard the gospel from Paul, the most anointed leader of the early Church.

Paul's chains were God's vehicle to bring the gospel to kings. Paul spoke with respect to leadership all the way through his trials. At each divine opportunity before the rulers, Paul gave his testimony. We never read of any bitterness toward God in Paul's testimonies; like many prophets before him, Paul was never disobedient to his vision:

> *And he said, Hear now my words: If there be a prophet among you, I the LORD will make myself known unto him in a vision, and will speak unto him in a dream. My servant Moses is not so, who is faithful in all mine house. With him will I speak mouth to mouth, even apparently, and not in dark speeches; and the similitude of the LORD shall he behold: wherefore then were ye not afraid to speak against my servant Moses?* (Numbers 12:6-8).

> *And the child Samuel ministered unto the LORD before Eli. And the word of the LORD was precious in those days; there was no open vision* (I Samuel 3:1).

I will stand upon my watch, and set me upon the tower, and will watch to see what he will say unto me, and what I shall answer when I am reproved. And the LORD answered me, and said, Write the vision, and make it plain upon tables, that he may run that readeth it. For the vision is yet for an appointed time, but at the end it shall speak, and not lie: though it tarry, wait for it; because it will surely come, it will not tarry (Habakkuk 2:1-3).

Where there is no vision, the people perish: but he that keepeth the law, happy is he (Proverbs 29:18).

People without a vision have no direction. When the prophets received their visions, they got their direction:

The Spirit of the Lord GOD is upon me; because the LORD hath anointed me to preach good tidings unto the meek; he hath sent me to bind up the brokenhearted, to proclaim liberty to the captives, and the opening of the prison to them that are bound; To proclaim the acceptable year of the LORD, and the day of vengeance of our God; to comfort all that mourn; To appoint unto them that mourn in Zion, to give unto them beauty for ashes, the oil of joy for mourning, the garment of praise for the spirit of heaviness; that they might be called trees of righteousness, the planting of the LORD, that he might be glorified. And they shall build the old wastes, they shall raise up the former desolations, and they shall repair the waste cities, the desolations of many generations (Isaiah 61:1-4).

And he said unto me, Son of man, stand upon thy feet, and I will speak unto thee. And the spirit entered into me when he spake unto me, and set me upon my feet, that I heard him that spake unto me (Ezekiel 2:1,2).

The Bible records seven visions given to Paul:

1. On the road to Damascus (Acts 9)

2. A trance at Jerusalem (Acts 22:17)

3. A vision of the third heaven (II Corinthians 12)

4. Paul's Macedonian call (Acts 16:9)

5. Encouragement at Corinth (Acts 18:9-11)

6. Paul told that he will go to Rome (Acts 23:11)

7. Encouragement in the storm (Acts 27:3)

PAUL'S ALTAR CALL

Paul was not just reciting a set of facts but preaching the gospel to the two men who stood before him. Paul's message included a call for repentance and good works:

. . . that they should repent and turn to God, and
do works meet for repentance (Acts 26:20).

Paul's message was nothing more than what Moses and
all the Jewish prophets had declared:

That Christ should suffer, and that he should be
the first that should rise from the dead, and
should shew light unto the people, and to the
Gentiles (Acts 26:23).

Festus declared Paul mad. Others had said the same thing
about Jesus. Festus could see only one world; Paul was in
touch with both worlds, the present world and the world
to come. Festus could not believe in resurrection, though
over 500 credible witnesses had seen Jesus after His death.

Agrippa knew Paul's message was true. Paul appealed to
Agrippa and sought a decision from this king. In response,
Paul heard the saddest words in the Bible:

. . . Almost thou persuadest me to be a Christian
(Acts 26:28).

If Agrippa would have become a Christian, he would have
been sneered at and looked down upon. It would have cost
him something, but to deny Christ cost Agrippa
everything—his very soul. There will come a day when it
will be Jesus Christ Who sits upon a throne, and Festus and
Agrippa will stand before Him on trial. For these two men
there will be no appeal to a higher power!

Paul's appeal to Caesar was already on record; and although Agrippa might have wanted to free him, God wanted Paul in Rome. Thus he would stand before the deranged son of Agrippina, the fifth emperor of the Roman Empire—Caesar Nero. But first Paul must survive a lethal storm at sea and a deadly snakebite!

CHAPTER THIRTEEN

Delivered!—Paul Defies Death To Appear in Rome
(Acts 27,28)

Does it sometimes feel as if circumstances are against what you know to be the will of God? What do you do at times like those? Give up? Forget the Lord's past leading and change your mind about God's will for you? Or do you stand upon the Word of God and use your stumbling blocks as stepping stones to higher ground? Despite all circumstances to the contrary, Paul knew that his destiny lay in Rome. Each obstacle (stonings, trials, imprisonment) only made Paul more determined to reach his goal. Let's look at why he felt that way:

> *After these things were ended, Paul purposed in the spirit, when he had passed through Macedonia and Achaia, to go to Jerusalem, saying, After I have been there, **I must also see Rome*** (Acts 19:21).

Making request, if by any means now at length I might have a prosperous journey by the will of God to come unto you. For I long to see you, . . . So, as much as in me is, **I am ready to preach the gospel to you that are at Rome also** (Romans 1:10,11,15).

And the night following the Lord stood by him, and said, Be of good cheer, Paul: for as thou hast testified of me in Jerusalem, **so must thou bear witness also at Rome** (Acts 23:11).

For if I be an offender, or have committed any thing worthy of death, I refuse not to die: but if there be none of these things whereof these accuse me, no man may deliver me unto them. **I appeal unto Caesar** (Acts 25:11).

For there stood by me this night the angel of God, whose I am, and whom I serve, Saying, Fear not, Paul; **thou must be brought before Caesar:** *and, lo, God hath given thee all them that sail with thee* (Acts 27:23,24).

Where we found brethren, and were desired to tarry with them seven days: and so **we went toward Rome** (Acts 28:14).

And when **we came to Rome,** *the centurion delivered the prisoners to the captain of the guard: but Paul was suffered to dwell by himself with a soldier that kept him* (Acts 28:16).

Paul's confidence to reach his final destination was in God's Word and God's leading in his spirit. What's your "Rome"? What goal or destination are you presently working toward? I believe that the Holy Spirit included the events in these last two chapters of Acts to encourage your faith and to assure you of God's presence in every circumstance of life.

PAUL'S FAITHFUL FRIENDS

Luke, no doubt, was with Paul during his stay in Caesarea; but he kept himself out of the narrative until the first verse of chapter 27. Notice that little word "we" that tells us of Luke's presence on Paul's journey to Rome:

And when it was determined that we should sail into Italy, they delivered Paul and certain other prisoners unto one named Julius, a centurion of Augustus' band (Acts 27:1).

Paul's other traveling companion was Aristarchus. We first met him while Paul was in Thessalonica:

And the whole city was filled with confusion: and having caught Gaius and Aristarchus, men of Macedonia, Paul's companions in travel, they rushed with one accord into the theatre (Acts 19:29).

And there accompanied him into Asia Sopater of Berea; and of the Thessalonians, Aristarchus and Secundus; and Gaius of Derbe, and Timotheus; and of Asia, Tychicus and Trophimus (Acts 20:4).

These men went with Paul to Jerusalem with the money given from the gentile churches. It is said that in order to accompany Paul to Rome, Luke and Aristarchus would have had to go as Paul's slaves. We do not know if this was actually the case, but it would certainly have shown their love.

When they reached the seaport of Sidon, Julius was very gracious to Paul and let him meet with his friends. In time, they sailed "under Cyprus" (refer to the map on page for locations mentioned in this chapter) and dropped anchor at Myra in the southern part of Asia Minor.

At Myra a change of ships was made. Egypt shipped much grain to the Roman Empire, and these grain ships were large. The centurion asked for space on the ship and transferred the prisoners. It took many days to sail from Myra to Fair Havens because they faced contrary winds.

Paul spoke up and issued a warning (by the direction of the Holy Spirit) of what was to come if they continued sailing. Luke says that " . . . *sailing was now dangerous, because the fast was now already past, . . .* " (Acts 27:9). This refers to Yom Kippur, the Day of Atonement, which is celebrated on the tenth day of the seventh month (Leviticus 23:27). This would be around October 1. The most dangerous times to sail were mid-September to mid-November. However, Paul's warnings were rejected; the centurion trusted in the word of man more than in the Word of God:

> *Nevertheless the centurion believed the master and the owner of the ship, more than those things which were spoken by Paul* (Acts 27:11).

They set sail with a deceptively smooth south wind, which changed to a violent wind. When we look in the gospels, we see that Jesus is with us even in the storm:

> *But the ship was now in the midst of the sea, tossed with waves: for the wind was contrary* (Matthew 14:24).

> *And he saw them toiling in rowing; for the wind was contrary unto them: and about the fourth watch of the night he cometh unto them, walking upon the sea, and would have passed by them* (Mark 6:48).

> *And when even was now come, his disciples went down unto the sea, And entered into a ship, and went over the sea toward Capernaum. And it was now dark, and Jesus was not come to them. And the sea arose by reason of a great wind that blew. So when they had rowed about five and twenty or thirty furlongs, they see Jesus walking on the sea, and drawing nigh unto the ship: and they were afraid. But he saith unto them, It is I; be not afraid. Then they willingly received him into the ship: and immediately the ship was at the*

land whither they went (John 6:16-21).

And the same day, when the even was come, he saith unto them, Let us pass over unto the other side. And when they had sent away the multitude, they took him even as he was in the ship. And there were also with him other little ships. And there arose a great storm of wind, and the waves beat into the ship, so that it was now full. And he was in the hinder part of the ship, asleep on a pillow: and they awake him, and say unto him, Master, carest thou not that we perish? And he arose, and rebuked the wind, and said unto the sea, Peace, be still. And the wind ceased, and there was a great calm. And he said unto them, Why are ye so fearful? how is it that ye have no faith? And they feared exceedingly, and said one to another, What manner of man is this, that even the wind and the sea obey him? (Mark 4:35-41).

STORM AT SEA

The sailors were afraid that they might be driven into some of the sand bars around the coast; the storm, however, took them out into the deep waters. The first day was a dreadful one. The next day, they had to throw out the cargo. On the third day they had to throw out the tackle—the sail and all the ship's furnishings. What could they do but throw themselves into the hands of God! God was permitting them to come to a place where they would believe and submit to His Word.

I am sure that the centurion, by this time, was sorry that he had believed the owner of the ship. He no doubt believed God now. Because of Paul's faith, an angel of God, a ministering spirit, came to minister to Paul in the storm:

> *For there stood by me this night the angel of God, whose I am, and whom I serve* (Acts 27:23).

> *Are they not all ministering spirits, sent forth to minister for them who shall be heirs of salvation?* (Hebrews 1:14).

Unsaved people certainly are blessed by being in the presence of saved people, and it should be that way. Potiphar was blessed because of Joseph:

> *And it came to pass from the time that he* [Potiphar] *had made him overseer in his house, and over all that he had, that the LORD blessed the Egyptian's house for Joseph's sake; and the blessing of the LORD was upon all that he had in the house, and in the field* (Genesis 39:5).

Laban was blessed because of Jacob:

> *For it was little which thou hadst before I came, and it is now increased unto a multitude; and the LORD hath blessed thee since my coming: and now when shall I provide for mine own house also?* (Genesis 30:30).

The passengers and prisoners were blessed because of

Paul. Today, the whole world is blessed because of the presence of the Church.

Paul told the ship's crew that they would be cast upon an island without any loss of life. On the "fourteenth night" (which might symbolize Passover—Exodus 12:1-6,11:4), about "midnight" (which might represent the end of the age—Matthew 25:1-13, Mark 13:35), the sailors knew they were near land. The spiritual lesson here is that full salvation comes through the Passover Lamb upon His Second Coming.

Paul encouraged all 276 persons aboard the ship to take bread and give thanks. Paul knew that God had told him that he would stand before Caesar. No matter what they went through, God had promised him. God wanted Caesar, one of the most wretched men who ever walked this earth, to hear the gospel—and to hear it through Paul's lips.

The sailors knew they were being driven to shore; the water was decreasing rapidly. They had to run the ship aground. The sailors decided that they would leave the ship in a small boat and let what would happen to the people happen. But Paul saw through what they were trying to do and told the centurion that if everyone didn't stay on the ship, they all wouldn't be saved. By this time the centurion had learned to listen to Paul, and the skiff was cut loose without anyone leaving the boat.

When they finally ran aground, the counsel of the soldiers was to kill the prisoners. This seems so cruel, but the Romans had a code that every Roman soldier was responsible personally for his prisoner. If a prisoner escaped, they gave their own lives in forfeit. They were afraid; but again the centurion, who was Paul's friend by now, was determined to save him. He commanded that all be allowed to swim to shore. All aboard the ship made it safely ashore to the island of Melita.

The word *Melita* is a Canaanite word that means "refuge." Today the island is called Malta. The islanders were very gracious in providing a fire to warm the shipwrecked travelers.

The devil had tried his best to drown Paul at sea, but Paul had a divine appointment at Rome. When drowning didn't work, the devil tried to eliminate Paul through a snakebite! Paul shook the snake into the fire, and the fact that he didn't die was a great sign to the islanders.

Publius, the head of the island, lodged Paul and his group for three days. When the father of Publius became sick, Paul laid hands on him and healed him. News of the miracle spread, and others from the island brought the sick to Paul:

> *So when this was done, others also, which had diseases in the island, came, and were healed* (Acts 28:9).

What a marvelous account of the gospel in action! Paul used the gift of healing to bless all who were sick on the island. Ministering healing to their bodies no doubt opened the way for ministry to their spirits. Never before in the book of Acts had Paul been so welcomed and so honored as he was here. Melita was truly a "refuge" for Paul.

Today, the church is a place of refuge for believers and unbelievers. For Christians it is a place of refuge from the daily contamination that results from being "in the world" but not "of it." Whenever you feel "out of it," depressed, lonely, or sick, *run* to church and take refuge in the presence of God and the fellowship of other saints!

For unbelievers, the church is the *only* refuge from the coming judgment. You and I need to lead others to this refuge. Like Paul, God has given us the authority to lay hands on the sick and to see them recover:

> *And these signs shall follow them that believe; In my name shall they cast out devils; they shall speak with new tongues; They shall take up serpents; and if they drink any deadly thing, it shall not hurt them; they shall lay hands on the sick, and they shall recover* (Mark 16:17,18).

Remember, the supernatural is not just so that you can have a big name. The supernatural lifts up the name of Jesus and provides an inroad for the preaching of the gospel. Step out in faith to those around you, and God will meet their *physical* and *spiritual* needs through YOU.

ROME AT LAST

At long last Paul and his group came to Rome. Immediately Paul began to witness to the Jews living in Rome. Jesus had told him to go to the uttermost parts of the earth, and Paul was about his Master's business.

Although there were thousands of Jews in the early Church, Paul's major opposition however came from the Jews. While a prisoner in Rome, Paul preached the gospel to the Jews there:

And when they had appointed him a day, there came many to him into his lodging; to whom he expounded and testified the kingdom of God, persuading them concerning Jesus, both out of the law of Moses, and out of the prophets, from morning till evening (Acts 28:23).

The reaction of the Jews was the same everywhere Paul had traveled:

And some believed the things which were spoken, and some believed not (Acts 28:24).

Paul's love for the Jews and their rejection of his good news must have saddened him much. Finally he spoke to them from the prophet Isaiah:

. . . Well spake the Holy Ghost by Esaias the prophet unto our father, Saying, Go unto this people, and say, Hearing ye shall hear, and shall not understand; and seeing ye shall see, and not perceive: For the heart of this people is waxed gross, and their ears are dull of hearing, and their eyes have they closed; lest they should see with their eyes, and hear with their ears, and understand with their heart, and should be converted, and I should heal them (Acts 28:25-27).

209

This prophecy is quoted five other times in the New Testament. Surely the Holy Spirit thinks its message is important:

Therefore speak I to them in parables: because they seeing see not; and hearing they hear not, neither do they understand (Matthew 13:13).

That seeing they may see, and not perceive; and hearing they may hear, and not understand; lest at any time they should be converted, and their sins should be forgiven them (Mark 4:12).

And he said, Unto you it is given to know the mysteries of the kingdom of God: but to others in parables; that seeing they might not see, and hearing they might not understand (Luke 8:10).

He hath blinded their eyes, and hardened their heart; that they should not see with their eyes, nor understand with their heart, and be converted, and I should heal them (John 12:40).

(According as it is written, God hath given them the spirit of slumber, eyes that they should not see, and ears that they should not hear;) unto this day (Romans 11:8).

Paul quoted the prophecy for the last time. This was the closing of the door—the day of the Jews' privilege was over. In a few short years, the Temple would be demolished and Jerusalem would be trodden down by the Romans.

PAUL'S PRISON MINISTRY

During Paul's first period of imprisonment, he wrote the books of the Bible that we now call Philippians, Ephesians, Colossians, and Philemon. Paul's incarceration was not wasted time, but time that would bless the Body of Christ forever. He won many to Christ; he had contacts right in Caesar's household:

All the saints salute you, chiefly they that are of Caesar's household (Philippians 4:22).

Paul might have been locked up, but he never shut up! Although he was imprisoned for a number of years, Paul was perhaps one of the greatest travelers of his day. He visited many lands and saw many new scenes in different countries. Some may find it strange that in all the letters Paul wrote he never once mentioned the scenery of the countries through which he passed. There is not one line in his letters telling of the wonders of the architecture of his day. Is there a reason for this? I believe it was because Paul was "blind." As he traveled about he was blind to all else but one thing. On the way to Damascus, when he met the Lord Jesus, he was blinded by the vision of Christ's great glory. From that time on he could see nothing but Jesus and tell of nothing but His gospel.

Jesus wants you and me to speak up boldly and to walk in the same glory and miracle-working power as Paul and the early Church. If we will believe as the early Church believed, then we will act as the early Church acted; then we will experience the same power and anointing as they did.

Jesus is coming back for a glorious Church; our prayer should be the same prayer for power spoken by the apostles in Acts 4:29,30: "Lord grant that Your servants with all boldness preach the Word, and that signs and wonders may be done in the name of Thy holy child Jesus. Amen!"

APPENDIX
OF MAPS

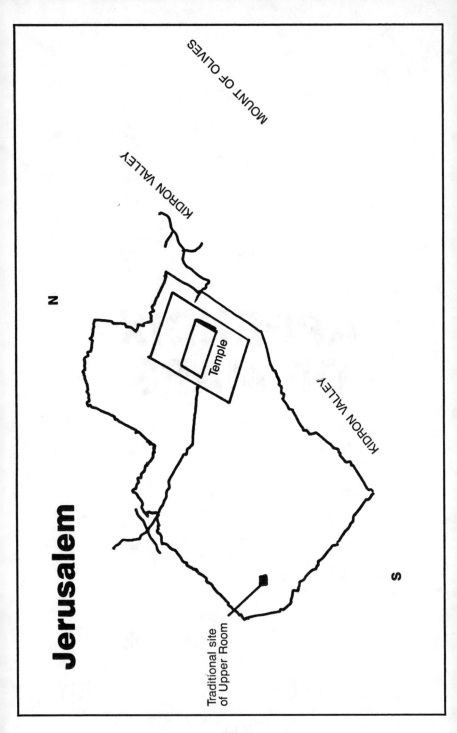

Jerusalem

MOUNT OF OLIVES

KIDRON VALLEY

N

S

KIDRON VALLEY

Temple

Traditional site
of Upper Room

214

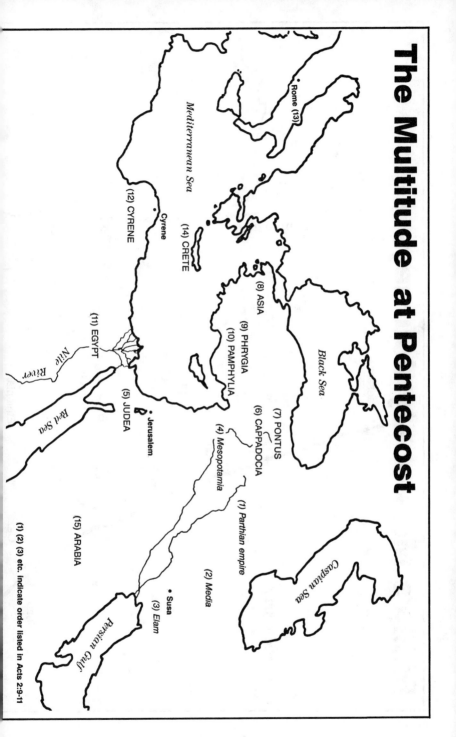

The Multitude at Pentecost

Rome (13)

Mediterranean Sea

(12) CYRENE

Cyrene

(14) CRETE

(8) ASIA

(9) PHRYGIA

(10) PAMPHYLIA

Black Sea

(7) PONTUS

(6) CAPPADOCIA

(11) EGYPT

Nile River

Red Sea

(5) JUDEA

Jerusalem

(4) Mesopotamia

(1) Parthian empire

(2) Media

Susa

(3) Elam

Caspian Sea

(15) ARABIA

Persian Gulf

(1) (2) (3) etc. indicate order listed in Acts 2:9-11

215

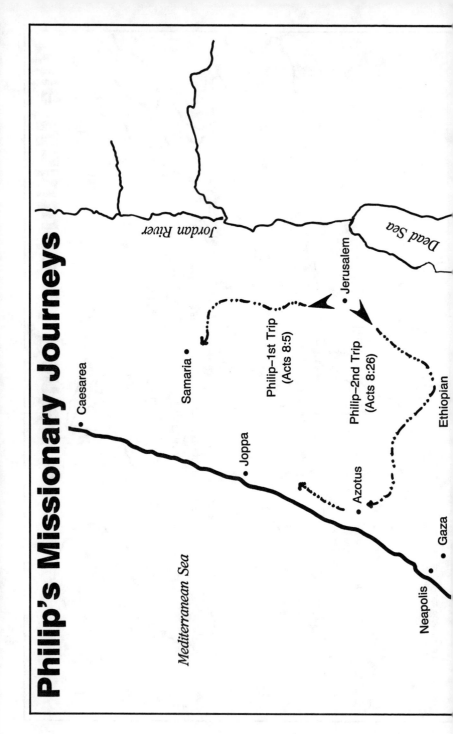

Philip's Missionary Journeys

Caesarea

Samaria

Philip–1st Trip
(Acts 8:5)

Philip–2nd Trip
(Acts 8:26)

Joppa

Azotus

Gaza

Neapolis

Ethiopian

Jerusalem

Jordan River

Dead Sea

Mediterranean Sea

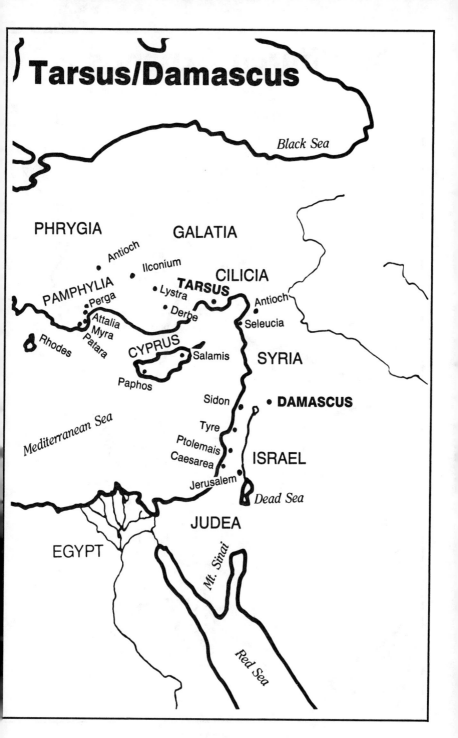

Tarsus/Damascus

Black Sea

PHRYGIA

GALATIA

Antioch

Ilconium

CILICIA

PAMPHYLIA

TARSUS

Perga

Lystra

Antioch

Attalia

Derbe

Myra

Seleucia

Rhodes

Patara

CYPRUS

Salamis

SYRIA

Paphos

Sidon

DAMASCUS

Mediterranean Sea

Tyre

Ptolemais

ISRAEL

Caesarea

Jerusalem

Dead Sea

JUDEA

Mt. Sinai

EGYPT

Red Sea

217

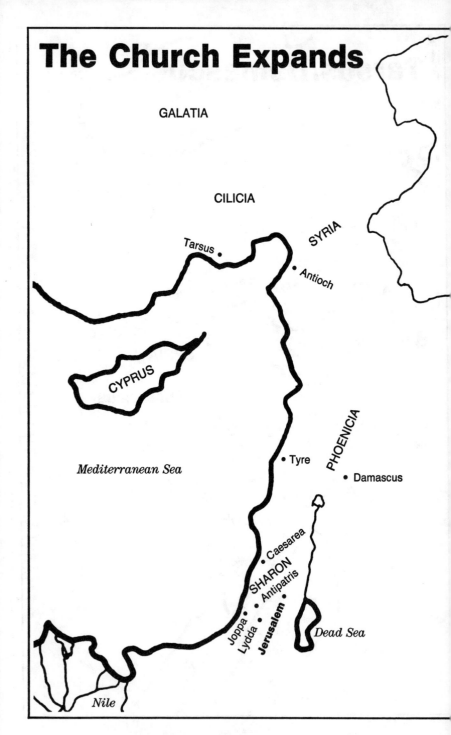

The Church Expands

GALATIA

CILICIA

Tarsus •

SYRIA

• Antioch

CYPRUS

Mediterranean Sea

PHOENICIA

• Tyre

• Damascus

• Caesarea

SHARON

• Antipatris

Joppa •

Lydda •

Jerusalem •

Dead Sea

Nile

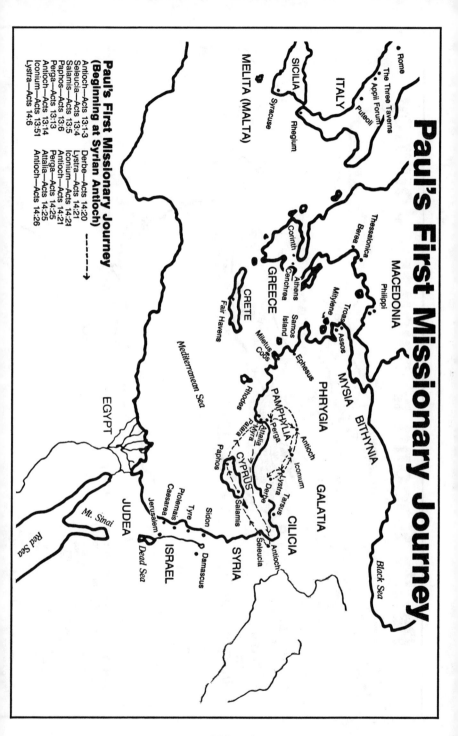

Paul's First Missionary Journey

Paul's First Missionary Journey (Beginning at Syrian Antioch)

Antioch—Acts 13:1-3
Seleucia—Acts 13:4
Salamis—Acts 13:5
Paphos—Acts 13:6
Perga—Acts 13:13
Antioch—Acts 13:14
Iconium—Acts 13:51
Lystra—Acts 14:6
Derbe—Acts 14:20
Lystra—Acts 14:21
Iconium—Acts 14:21
Antioch—Acts 14:21
Perga—Acts 14:25
Attalia—Acts 14:25
Antioch—Acts 14:26

-------->

219

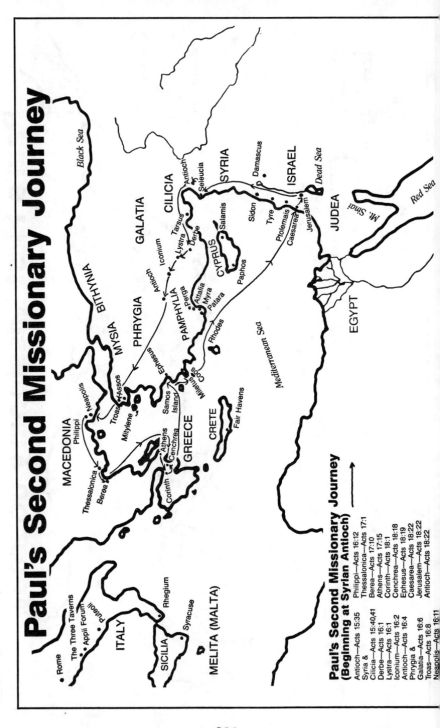

Paul's Second Missionary Journey

Paul's Second Missionary Journey
(Beginning at Syrian Antioch) ⟶

Antioch—Acts 15:35
Syria &
Cilicia—Acts 15:40,41
Derbe—Acts 16:1
Lystra—Acts 16:1
Iconium—Acts 16:2
Antioch—Acts 16:4
Phrygia &
Galatia—Acts 16:6
Troas—Acts 16:8
Neapolis—Acts 16:11

Philippi—Acts 16:12
Thessalonica—Acts 17:1
Berea—Acts 17:10
Athens—Acts 17:15
Corinth—Acts 18:1
Cenchrea—Acts 18:18
Ephesus—Acts 18:19
Caesarea—Acts 18:22
Jerusalem—Acts 18:22
Antioch—Acts 18:22

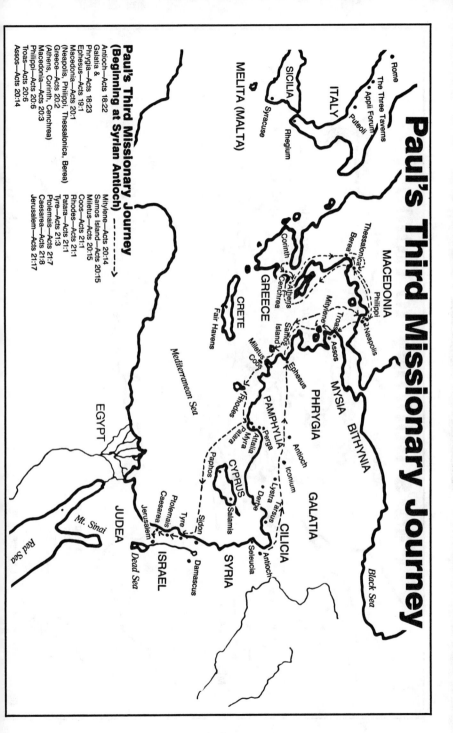

Paul's Third Missionary Journey

Paul's Third Missionary Journey (Beginning at Syrian Antioch) ----->

Antioch—Acts 18:22
Galatia &
Phrygia—Acts 18:23
Ephesus—Acts 19:1
Macedonia—Acts 20:1
(Neapolis, Philippi, Thessalonica, Berea)
Greece—Acts 20:2
(Athens, Corinth, Cenchrea)
Macedonia—Acts 20:3
Philippi—Acts 20:6
Troas—Acts 20:6
Assos—Acts 20:14

Mitylene—Acts 20:14
Samos Island—Acts 20:15
Miletus—Acts 20:15
Coos—Acts 21:1
Rhodes—Acts 21:1
Patara—Acts 21:1
Tyre—Acts 21:3
Ptolemais—Acts 21:7
Caesarea—Acts 21:8
Jerusalem—Acts 21:17

221

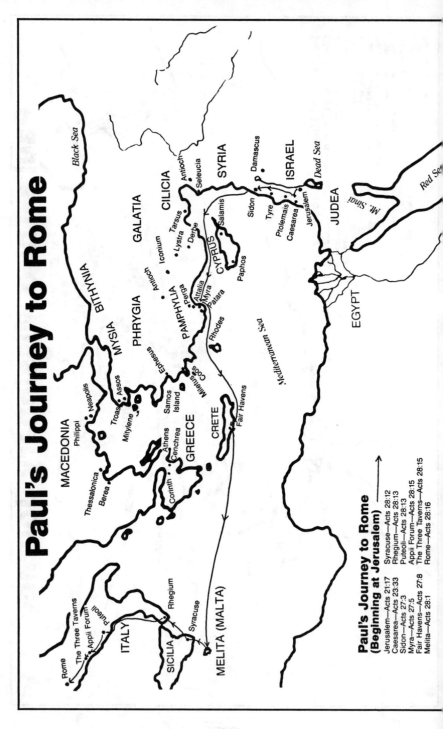

Paul's Journey to Rome

Paul's Journey to Rome
(Beginning at Jerusalem)

Jerusalem—Acts 21:17
Caesarea—Acts 23:33
Sidon—Acts 27:3
Myra—Acts 27:5
Fair Havens—Acts 27:8
Melita—Acts 28:1

Syracuse—Acts 28:12
Rhegium—Acts 28:13
Puteoli—Acts 28:13
Appii Forum—Acts 28:15
The Three Taverns—Acts 28:15
Rome—Acts 28:16

BIBLIOGRAPHY

Conner, Kevin J. ACTS. Portland: Bible Temple, 1973.
Dake, Finis Jennings. DAKE'S ANNOTATED
  REFERENCE BIBLE. Lawrenceville: Dake Bible
  Sales, Inc., 1963.
Lockyer, Herbert Sr. NELSON'S ILLUSTRATED BIBLE
  DICTIONARY. Nashville: Thomas Nelson Publishers,
  1986.
Phillips, John. EXPLORING ACTS. Vols. 1,2. Chicago:
  Moody Press, 1986.
Strong, James. STRONG'S EXHAUSTIVE CONCORDANCE
  COMPACT EDITION. Grand Rapids: Baker Book
  House, 1981.
Wilkinson, Bruce and Kenneth Boa. TALK THRU THE
  BIBLE. Nashville: Thomas Nelson Publishers, 1983.
  _____. THE BETHANY PARALLEL
  COMMENTARY ON THE NEW TESTAMENT.
  Minneapolis: Bethany House Publishers, 1983.

Receive Jesus Christ as Lord and Savior of Your Life.

The Bible says, "That if thou shalt confess with thy mouth the Lord Jesus, and shalt believe in thine heart that God hath raised him from the dead, thou shalt be saved. For with the heart man believeth unto righteousness; and with the mouth confession is made unto salvation" (Romans 10:9,10).

To receive Jesus Christ as Lord and Savior of your life, sincerely pray this prayer from your heart:

Dear Jesus,

I believe that You died for me and that You rose again on the third day. I confess to You that I am a sinner and that I need Your love and forgiveness. Come into my life, forgive my sins, and give me eternal life. I confess You now as my Lord. Thank You for my salvation!

Signed _____

Date _____

Write to us.

We will send you information to help you with your new life in Christ.

Marilyn Hickey Ministries • P.O. Box 17340
Denver, CO 80217 • (303) 770-0400

BOOKS BY MARILYN HICKEY

A CRY FOR MIRACLES ($5.95)
ACTS ($7.95)
ANGELS ALL AROUND ($7.95)
BEAT TENSION ($.75)
BE HEALED ($8.95)
BIBLE CAN CHANGE YOU, THE ($12.95)
BOLD MEN WIN ($.75)
BREAK THE GENERATION CURSE ($7.95)
BULLDOG FAITH ($.75)
CHANGE YOUR LIFE ($.75)
CHILDREN WHO HIT THE MARK ($.75)
CONQUERING SETBACKS ($.75)
DAILY DEVOTIONAL ($5.95)
DEAR MARILYN ($5.95)
DIVORCE IS NOT THE ANSWER ($4.95)
ESPECIALLY FOR TODAY'S WOMAN ($14.95)
EXPERIENCE LONG LIFE ($.75)
FASTING & PRAYER ($.75)
FREEDOM FROM BONDAGES ($4.95)
GIFT-WRAPPED FRUIT ($2.00)
GOD'S BENEFIT: HEALING ($.75)
GOD'S COVENANT FOR YOUR FAMILY ($5.95)
GOD'S RX FOR A HURTING HEART ($3.50)
GOD'S SEVEN KEYS TO MAKE YOU RICH ($.75)
HOLD ON TO YOUR DREAM ($.75)
HOW TO BE A MATURE CHRISTIAN ($5.95)
HOW TO BECOME MORE THAN A CONQUEROR ($.75)
HOW TO WIN FRIENDS ($.75)
I CAN BE BORN AGAIN AND SPIRIT FILLED ($.75)
I CAN DARE TO BE AN ACHIEVER ($.75)
KEYS TO HEALING REJECTION ($.75)
KNOW YOUR MINISTRY ($3.50)
MAXIMIZE YOUR DAY . . . GOD'S WAY ($7.95)
NAMES OF GOD ($7.95)
#1 KEY TO SUCCESS—MEDITATION, THE ($3.50)
POWER OF FORGIVENESS, THE ($.75)
POWER OF THE BLOOD, THE ($.75)
RECEIVING RESURRECTION POWER ($.75)
RENEW YOUR MIND ($.75)
SATAN-PROOF YOUR HOME ($7.95)
"SAVE THE FAMILY" PROMISE BOOK ($14.95)
SIGNS IN THE HEAVENS ($5.95)
SOLVING LIFE'S PROBLEMS ($.75)
SPEAK THE WORD ($.75)
STANDING IN THE GAP ($.75)
STORY OF ESTHER, THE ($.75)
TITHES • OFFERINGS • ALMS /
   GOD'S PLAN FOR BLESSING YOU ($.75)
WINNING OVER WEIGHT ($.75)
WOMEN OF THE WORD ($.75)
YOUR MIRACLE SOURCE ($3.50)
YOUR PERSONALITY WORKOUT ($5.95)

Prayer Requests

**Let us join our faith with yours
for your prayer needs. Fill out below
and send to**

**Marilyn Hickey Ministries
P.O. Box 17340
Denver, CO 80217**

Prayer Request_____

_____

_____

_____

_____

_____

Name ^{Mr. & Mrs.} ^{Mr.} ^{Miss} ^{Mrs.}_____

Address_____

City_____

State_____ Zip _____

Phone (H) (   ) _____

(W) (   ) _____

MARILYN

HICKEY

BIBLE

COLLEGE

Explore your options and increase your knowledge of the Word at this unique college of higher learning for men and women of faith. The Marilyn Hickey Bible College offers **on-campus and correspondence courses** that give you the opportunity to learn from Marilyn Hickey and other great Bible scholars, who can help prepare you to be an effective minister of the gospel. Classes are available for both full- and part-time students.

For more information, complete the coupon below and send to

**Marilyn Hickey Bible College
P.O. Box 17340
Denver, CO 80217
(303) 770-0400**

Name ^{Mr.} ^{Mrs.} ^{Miss} _____ Please print.

Address_____

City _____ State _____ Zip _____

Phone (H) ( ) _____ (W) ( ) _____

For Your Information
Free Monthly Magazine

☐ Please send me your free monthly magazine
OUTPOURING (including daily devotionals,
timely articles, and ministry updates)!

Tapes and Books

☐ Please send me Marilyn's latest product catalog.

Mr. & Mrs.
Miss
Mrs.
Name Mr._____ Please print.

Address _____

City_____

State_____ Zip _____

Phone (H) (   ) _____

       (W) (   ) _____

Mail to
Marilyn Hickey Ministries
P.O. Box 17340
Denver, CO 80217
(303) 770-0400